To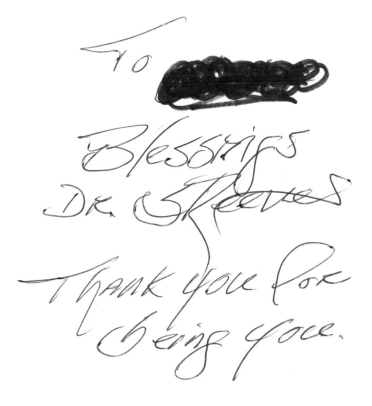

Blessings
Dr. Reeves

Thank you for
being you.

What Others Are Saying
About Shirlene Reeves and *Selling Through Your Heart*

"Shirlene Reeves has written an excellent book that will open your eyes to the opportunities all around you. Because she comes from the heart, she doesn't have to sell like ordinary people. She'll show you how she does it."

— Robert G. Allen
#1 *New York Times* Bestselling Author

"It is everyone's dream to be financially secure and self-sufficient. In this busy world, everyone is looking for a shortcut to achieve this goal. Now there is a way to obtain this by reading this incredible book about redefining and enabling one to achieve financial success. This is a must-read! The techniques you will learn in this book will enable you and your family to lead a joyous, profitable life."

— Dr. Michael Gross
Professional Keynote Speaker, Life Coach,
Entrepreneur, and Author of *The Spiritual Primer*

"It doesn't matter whether you've been selling for years or you are new to sales and just starting your business. *Selling Through Your Heart* will make a massive difference in your income. I think the content suits every entrepreneur. Anyone looking for the answers that will support them in getting their clients to say yes in a way that makes them feel good and you feel confident can't go wrong with this book."

— Linda Wells,
Speaker, Author, and Men's Anxiety Expert

"I'm impressed with Shirlene because she's already built a big business and she walks her talk, so she's definitely qualified to teach the things small business owners need to know. What I got from this amazing book was a step-by-step formula for what I needed to do to build relationships with others to increase my income and grow my business. I'm a complete introvert, so this book was really helpful. I needed to know exactly what to do to grow my business, and I'm over-the-top excited about the results I'm already beginning to receive."

— Angeline Hart,
Gorilla Love Coach & Author of *Gorillas Make Great Lovers!*

"This is an amazing book full of step-by-step information. I was surprised by how the techniques in *Selling Through Your Heart* took my life, my work, and my relationships to a whole new level of success and fulfillment. The content in this book is the perfect reference guide for me to go back to over and over again, and the business blueprint lays out an easy path to follow. Best of all, my income has really jumped up and my business is becoming massively visible, too."

— Dot Claire,
Modern Day Medicine Woman—Video Blogs on Aging Young

"Shirlene has risen from the depths of despair to the heights of success through entrepreneurship. If you want to learn how to avoid the pitfalls and follow in her footsteps, this reveal-all book is for you."

— Laura Rubinstein, CHt,
Bestselling Author and Digital Media & Marketing Strategist
at TransformToday.com

"I didn't realize how automatic and sales-y my old responses were to potential clients until I learned the sales techniques in Shirlene's book. They've made a huge difference in my business, and I'm much more aware of how others relate to me now. When I was practicing at a networking event, this guy asked me for my card and then chased me across the room asking whether we could work together. Usually, I have to chase everyone, but now everything has changed. This book is amazing. I'd highly recommend it to anyone who needs to sell to make a living."

— Carol Dysart,
Entrepreneur, Speaker, Founder of PeopleSmart World, &
DISC Master

"Shirlene's fabulous book really dives into how to build the right relationships that produce immediate and long-term benefits for any entrepreneur or sales rep. Grab a copy and start transforming the way you 'go after' your next sale!"

— Tonya Hofmann,
CEO and Founder of the Public Speakers Association http://publicspeakersassociation.com

"I've never known any teacher or mentor on improving personal effectiveness to generate such an overwhelmingly positive reaction. This book captures beautifully Shirlene's philosophy of principles. I think anyone reading it will quickly understand the enormous reaction I and others have had to Shirlene Reeves' teachings."

— James Hardy,
CEO eVantage Financial

"I love this book because it taught me how to market and sell in a way that doesn't make me feel bad or pushy. Shirlene totally comes from the heart and has taught me how to connect with people in a way that fits my style authentically. Now I have the secret to refining what I think and say about my business in a way that's professional but still very warm and nurturing. I would recommend this book to any coach searching for the answers for building a business and making more sales."

— Milea Schneider,
Entrepreneur, Health & Wellness Coach

"Shirlene Reeves and her book *Selling Through Your Heart* is exactly what this country needs right now. We are always waiting for the government or elected officials to do something for us and our livelihood. Shirlene shows us how to be self-sufficient, master our business, and ttake charge of the direction for our own lives. If you're an entrepreneur, business owner, or someone frustrated with the instability of working for someone else, you must read this book now!"

— James W. Connolly,
President/CEO of CEO Chef Consulting, Speaker, and Author of
*Creating Leaders to Build Teams: Aligning Your Purpose Toward a
Winning Work Culture*

"Before, I was all over the place, spinning my wheels, but now because I read Shirlene Reeves' book, I've pinpointed my target market and developed a speech that speaks directly to the people I want to work with and the people who need me. What a difference in my sales and my income. I just sold a $30,000 program. This book changed everything for me."

— Dr. Debra Dupree,
Entrepreneur, Speaker, & Owner of Relationships At Work

"If you're a serious entrepreneur and want to perform at a Level 10/10 to be the 'Best Version of You' authentically, *Selling Through Your Heart* is the book for you. Shirlene has the most compelling and thought-provoking, motivational and inspirational information for you to truly be a successful entrepreneur. Shirlene delivers this in every chapter in as elegant and graceful a way as she would in person."

— Dr. Renee Michelle Gordon
Speaker, Love & Relationship Coach, and Author of *Finding Your Love at Last: Five Simple Steps to Attracting Your Soulmate*

"BRILLIANT! What I loved about this amazing book is that it really catered to my style of connecting with people, and I think it would be great for everybody. I'm really excited that I get to be authentic in the sales process and don't need to memorize any scripts."

— Moneeka Sawyer,
Entrepreneur, Speaker, & Author of *Choose Bliss*

"Shirlene Reeves has coalesced a step-by-step system so you can achieve living a life that is self-empowered, effective, and amazingly productive. This is not some ivory tower philosophical approach. The tools were tempered on her own personal hardship, diligent work, and phenomenal success. You will have to do the work, dig deep, and come to terms with yourself. When you follow her advice in *Selling Through Your Heart* and do the integrated exercises, you will find yourself in control of your destiny. Happiness, success, and living through love will then be yours to command. Lucky you!"

— Neal Katz,
Award-Winning Author of the Victoria Woodhull Saga

"Be prepared to be blown away by the *Selling Through Your Heart* business and sales formula. I connected with Shirlene only once on the phone, but I knew immediately that she was the person I wanted to work with. Now, after taking her courses and reading this remarkable book, I'm blown away by the tools I've been given."

— Annie Pool,
Entrepreneur, Speaker, & Author of
Passport to Life: How I Overcame Incurable Cancer

"A must-read book for anyone is sales! Shirlene has captured a very simple but powerful formula for achieving tremendous business success. She takes you by the hand and gives you the knowledge, confidence, and power to achieve your sales goals."

— Teresa de Grosbois,
#1 International Bestselling Author of
Mass Influence: The Habits of the Highly Influential

"The secret of Shirlene Reeves' wonderful book can be found in the title: *Selling With Your Heart: Empowering You to Build Relationships for Financial Freedom.* These strategies work because someone from the front lines with years of experience is mentoring you. This book will be forever around, helping, teaching, and empowering."

— Patrick Snow,
Publishing Coach and International Best-Selling Author
of *Creating Your Own Destiny*

"If you want to develop the mindset of a winner in the entrepreneurial arena, you've found the answer. All I want to know is where was this insightful book when I got started in the business world?"

— Debbi Dachinger,
Award-Winning Syndicated Radio Personality, International Bestselling Author, Media Coach, & Red Carpet Correspondent

"Finally, someone who understands the sleepless angst and confusion caused by the pursuit of sales and building a business. If you have spent futile time trying to memorize scripts attempting to get the sales process right...Shirlene Reeves book, *Selling Through Your Heart,* will change your world. This amazing book teaches the secrets for selling authentically, by using your own words so that you can easily have sales and business success."

— Paula Shaw
Grief and Trauma Expert, Transition Radio Co-Host

"If you want to know the secrets to maximizing your business and your wealth, there's nobody better than Shirlene Reeves to reveal them. This book defines how to increase your business income, become visible worldwide, and make a big impact in the world."

— Neal Sperling,
Entrepreneur & World-Class Connector

"I believe everyone is ultimately seeking financial freedom. This book is powerful because Shirlene Reeves takes you down a unique path of redefining what it means to own an 'income-generating' business and finally get out of the 'hobby zone.' If it's your time to make an impact with your business, this book is your new guide to financial freedom."

— Steven P.A. Keener, D.C.

"Shirlene Reeves' track record for success, with so many entrepreneurs, shows that her principles are universally effective. In this book, she gives you a clear and concise roadmap for achieving more success than you would ever think possible. If you follow it, you're sure to get there."

— Harrison Klein,
Transformationalist, Author, Teacher, & World Thought Leader

"Throughout my nearly forty years of being in classrooms training entrepreneurs, professionals, coaches, and people from many walks of life, I've found without question that sales and marketing systems are the keys to success...but even more importantly, building relationships is the key to making a great living—having a lucrative lifestyle—and ultimately reaching financial freedom. This book is a must read.... Shirlene's inherent wisdom and practicality from years of being 'in the trenches' will empower and support you to achieve the success you have been searching for. Take these ideas and run with them for the sake of your business, your financial success, and your goals—and if you are committed to the betterment of humanity—for all of us!"

— Dame DC Cordova
CEO/Owner, Excellerated Business Schools®/Money & You®

"*Selling Through Your Heart* is the kind of book everyone can benefit from who wants to take his or her business to the next level. I loved learning the 3 Step Sales Waltz™ and how to apply it to my business so I can convince clients they need me without being pushy or scaring them off. Plus, Shirlene's advice on how to create multiple streams of income is worth ten times the price of this book easily."

— Tyler R. Tichelaar, PhD
Award-Winning Author of *Narrow Lives* and *The Best Place*

"This book hits the mark. With powerful, practical, fear-conquering advice, you learn what it takes to master your own game of business, and thrive in every area of your life—no matter what your age. Shirlene demystifies the sales and wealth-generating process with clear, concise, uplifting, confidence-boosting wisdom gleaned from her own trial and error life experiences."

— Susan Friedmann,
CSP, International Bestselling Author of *Riches in Niches:
How to Make It BIG in a small Market*

"Shirlene has done it! The insights in *Selling Through Your Heart* is exactly what entrepreneurs need to increase profits and live an amazing lifestyle. This book is full of insights and wisdom that empowers the reader to create a successful business no matter how many failures he or she may have had in the past. Truly, this book is a tremendous resource for any business owner who wants to generate consistent cash flow."

— Ken D Foster,
Best-Selling Author, Radio Show Host

"*Selling Through Your Heart* provides a comprehensive and sustainable approach to navigating the sales process authentically. It's destined to become 'the handbook' for those wishing to master the skill of sales to produce extraordinary results. Shirlene Reeves has left nothing out as she combines decades of business wisdom with a fresh approach to selling that is easy to read, comprehend, and practice."

— Kathy Fairbanks
Director of Client Solutions, Klemmer & Associates
Leadership Seminars, Inc., Host at Voice America World Talk Radio
for *The Compassionate Samurai Business Hour*

"In *Selling Through Your Heart*, Shirlene Reeves has provided many books in one, each amazingly valuable. Whether you are on your first entrepreneurial foray, or enriching the business you have, she reminds you that authenticity must underlie every step. Building on that firm foundation, she systematically shows you how to align your dreams, your vision, your plans and practices with practical spiritual principles to build a thriving business you love. What could be better!"

— Rhoberta Shaler, PhD
The Relationship Help Doctor, ForRelationshipHelp.com

"In her wonderful book, *Selling with Your Heart: Empowering You to Build Relationships for Financial Freedom,* Shirlene Reeves helps us to realize that the secret to success, not only in business but in all areas of our lives, is to believe in our heart-felt dreams; courageously following what may seem to be impossible. Through her diligence, hard work, and by changing the nature of herself to become one of belief, trust, and faith, the miraculous occurred in not only the monetary riches of her world, but in the great wealth of ultimately knowing who she Divinely is."

— Claire Candy Hough
1 Amazon International Bestselling Author of
I Am an Angelic Walk-In, CEO Angel Healing House,
Radio/TV Host, Inspirational Speaker

"*Selling Through Your Heart* is an incredible gift! Shirlene Reeves grew a company from 0 to 23,000 team members and multiple millions of dollars in revenue. Then she lost it all, and ended up considering a dumpster dive to feed her two young boys. A year later, she had grown it all back and more by using her time-tested technique of selling through your heart. This isn't just a book; it's a transformational experience!"

— Seth Greene, CEO Market Domination LLC,
the Only 3X Marketer of the Year Nominee, and
Best-Selling Author of Seven Marketing Books

"In her book *Selling Through Your Heart*, Shirlene Reeves marries the best of both worlds from her immense storehouse of knowledge and experience—entrepreneurial business acceleration from a heart-based perspective and wealthy building. Her book will upgrade your mindset, your systems, your confidence, and your actions in order to improve your sales mastery, make you massively visible, and catapult your revenue. You can't afford to miss this one!"

— Jackie Lapin, Founder of SpeakerTunity.com

"Sales is such a wonderful profession, but many people struggle to have repeatable and consistent success. Shirlene has done an excellent job of outlining the theory behind why, and then the specific tactics you need to take to help you reach the sales goals you desire! There are lots of great tidbits and action-oriented ideas to choose from."

— Bev Flaxington, The Human Behavior Coach®

"I love Shirlene's passion and heart. Her book will help you develop a business plan that supports your business, you, and your mission. *Selling Through Your Heart* shares the techniques to achieve both increased visibility and sell from the heart powerfully. Discovering how to do this will support you in stepping into the impact, income, and reach you are called to do so you can shine powerfully in the world."

"This book has it all! It contains everything an entrepreneur must know in order to launch a successful business. Those who have been struggling to get their businesses off the ground will also benefit greatly from Shirlene's practical, easy-to-follow guidance. From social media wizardry to networking mastery, Shirlene offers powerful ways to market you and your business, not just locally, but globally! As a highly skilled and certified financial expert with decades of experience, she provides excellent advice for increasing your revenue stream, managing your profits, and budgeting your expenses. This is the only business reference guide you will ever need to launch and grow your business into a wildly successful company that will make a powerful and positive difference in the lives of many. By applying the wisdom, tools, and principles in Shirlene's book, you too can become a global difference maker!"

"When you change the way you look at things,
the things you look at change."

— Dr. Wayne Dyer

SELLING
THROUGH YOUR
Heart

EMPOWERING YOU
TO BUILD RELATIONSHIPS
FOR FINANCIAL FREEDOM

SHIRLENE REEVES

AVIVA
PUBLISHING
New York

To my father, Wayne Albert Meyer

Your greatest gift is your belief in my dreams and goals. There were times when even I wasn't clear on my vision, but you have always been there to hold the space with love, support, and encouragement for me. I promise you I will make every effort to share with others the beliefs, strengths, and blessings you have shared with me. Your strong values are in every fiber of my being, and your legacy lives on in all the lives you have touched. I love you. I am grateful for you. Thank you, Dad, for believing in me and continuing to be my rock.

Acknowledgments

No book is written alone. I have numerous people to thank, beginning with those whose own writings and sayings have inspired me throughout the years:

The Buddha, the Seven Beloved Masters, Jesus Christ, the Dalai Lama, Jack Canfield, Dale Carnegie, Stephen R. Covey, Dr. John Demartini, Teresa de Grosbois, T. Howard Howell, Aurora Louise Jones, Anne Katherine, Harrison Klein, Ryan Levesque, John C. Maxwell, Dr. Michael Newton, Tony Robbins, David J. Schwartz, Steven Scott, Michael A. Singer, Eckhart Tolle, Brian Tracy, Thomas Troward, Marianne Williamson, and Zig Ziglar.

With deepest appreciation and gratitude, I thank Robert G. Allen for writing his book, *Multiple Steams of Income*. The strategies in his book changed the course of my life, and today, they continue to provide my clients and me with safety and financial freedom.

To the late Wayne Dyer, I humbly thank you for your beautiful teachings and guidance on my path of spiritual growth while living on Maui. I don't go a day without remembering your message, "If you change the way you look at things, the things you look at change." I miss you, dear one.

To Ram Dass, for your guidance and the many intuitive gifts you imparted to me while sitting at your feet on the cliffs of Maui's North Shore. Your teachings on looking within to find the answers for how to live in this world created for me a life of peace and a clear understanding of how the universe works. I respectfully thank your soul for the gifts you've imparted to me and to the many humans you've guided.

Thank you to my son, Jason Akatiff: I am so proud of you and the loving, generous, successful man you've become. I encourage you to continue following your passion while always remembering that love of family comes first. Know that wherever you are is where you are meant to be. I love you, and I'm grateful that you are part of my life.

A big thank you to Carol Dysart and Sandra Davis of PeopleSmart World for providing support in the development of the DISC Sales program and Dr. Tony Alessandra, who created and provides the DISC online assessment program.

Thank you to Diana Cliver, who has supported and assisted my businesses and me for over twenty years. She has been by my side, treating my companies as her own in each step toward my success. I consider Diana to be the backbone of my company's growth, credibility, and accomplishments. Diana, you are truly an amazing soul.

A big thanks to Patrick Snow, who lit a fire under me to bring this book to fruition and point the way toward my next steps in massive visibility.

Contents

"You are not your mind. Whatever it says, don't fight with it. Don't try to change it. Just decide that no matter what it says, you are not getting involved. Thoughts and feelings are not you."

— Michael A. Singer

♡

Foreword

BY DR. JOHN DEMARTINI

I vividly remember a time in my life when I was a homeless surfer, living on the north shore of Oahu, Hawaii, when I had an epiphany that I could overcome my learning challenges and become a powerful teacher sharing my message with millions. This changed my life, and since then, I have been able to dedicate my life to full-time researching, writing, traveling, and teaching around the world.

What I've learned about life and business over the last forty-five years has been inspiring and deeply meaningful....

I began to ask: Why do some people achieve greatness and higher levels of fulfillment and others don't?

What I discovered was that high-achieving individuals have the ability to break through their self-imposed limitations to wake up and release the hidden and dormant genius within themselves. This waking up allows for a change in perception and an ability to tap into their inner resources that others may not realize they have. Because everyone doesn't know how to tap into those resources, people often flounder in trying to build their businesses and achieve greatness. What those inner resources are is really just being in touch with who you truly are, and once you make that contact with your true self, then you will discover the will and the burning desire to achieve the greatness you desire and feel you deserve. This discovery leads to amazing and authentic business achievements and inner fulfillment, or what Shirlene Reeves calls "selling through your heart."

In this powerful book by Shirlene, you will learn how to become one of those high-achieving individuals. You will discover how to funnel your genius with Shirlene's focused and easy-to-implement 3 Step Sales Waltz™. By using this method, you will learn how to build heart-based relationships with clients who will benefit from your expertise, keep buying from you, and recommend you to others.

In addition, Shirlene will teach you how to achieve in and empower all aspects of your business career. Her twenty-eight-year, time-tested, step-by-step strategy for building relationships will have you networking like you never did before. You'll learn the secret to creating powerful programs with appropriately priced marketing techniques. You'll be able to create effective solutions for increased visibility and massive sales, and perhaps greatest of all, you'll learn how to develop multiple streams of income so you can achieve a lifetime of financial freedom and have the time to do the things you most consistently and persistently desire.

Normally, it takes a minimum of three years to build a business, develop a referral base, and make an ordinary income. In *Selling Through Your Heart*, Shirlene Reeves offers a simple blueprint that will cut the time in half by eliminating unnecessary expenses, burnout, and lost revenue.

Most importantly, you will learn that you are ultimately the drive to your own business achievement. No one can sell your product better than you or establish stronger relationships with your clients than you, and no one can determine what your specific achievement will look like for you except you. Let Shirlene be your driving force to assist you in discovering exactly what you want your most inspiring achievement to look like and then show you what actions to take to make that great and unique achievement your reality.

So get ready for an amazing ride because when you learn to sell through your heart, not only will your bank balance grow, but you'll establish meaningful relationships that will make your inner and outer fulfillment quota skyrocket!

https://drdemartini.com/dr_demartini
http://maximizeyourwealthnow.com/dr-john-demartini/

FREE VIDEO DOWNLOADS

As a gift to you for reading this book, Shirlene is providing twenty FREE downloads, including videos and pdf reports on business, finance, and sales as a bonus with additional insights. You may go to the website ShirleneReeves.com to receive your gift. Just click on the FREE STUFF page under References.

Thank you for your interest in your own business, sales, and financial education.

INTRODUCTION

A Compelling Business Invitation

You're living off of your 401k, draining all of your savings, running from one networking group to another, and still, you're broke. It's been two years, and you've tried everything you heard the coaches standing on stage say, but it still isn't working. The dream of being your own boss and becoming an entrepreneur is quickly closing in on you, and then someone says, "You're going to have to get a J-O-B." You're feeling burnt out and depressed. *A job? No way!* you think. *Well, maybe that's exactly what I'll have to do if I don't make some money fast.*

How is your new title as an entrepreneur working out for you? Have you hit burnout yet? How's the money holding up? Are you headed for a J-O-B just to put gas in your car and food on the table? Have you been feeling overwhelmed by all the different ways you could build your business, so you're having trouble deciding which path to take? Are you tired of working endless hours every day trying to do the "right" things for your business, only to feel frustrated because you're in the same position you were in last month, and the month before, and the month before that?

I feel your pain. I have been in your shoes. I know what it's like to live in fear and wonder where your next meal will come from. There was a time in my life when I was standing in front of a big, green dumpster holding my two young children's tiny hands. As we stood there watching others dumpster-diving for watermelons, I could feel the fear rise up in my core. I had only fifteen cents in my pocket, and a pot of rice and beans was waiting for us in our tiny eighteen-foot trailer parked on the beach. It was one of the worst experiences of my life, but it is one I'll always remember.

At the point of desperation, it's not money we need nearly as much as we need knowledge, and it's knowledge you'll find in the pages that follow. You've already heard from all those other coaches what you're supposed to do to build your business and why, but so far it's all been a miserable failure.

Perhaps, like me, you've noticed that no one tells you how to build your business to create a successful income. Isn't that what you pay coaches and seminar leaders the big bucks for? I've decided to break all the rules of secrecy by providing you with the much-needed *how*.

Finally, you'll be given the secrets all of the coaches on stage leave out. After all, the information given to you from the stages was free, wasn't it? What did you expect? I guarantee that after reading this book and putting the assignments into action, you'll no longer need to waste your weekends crammed into tiny chairs, hoping for a nugget of information on how to make a living as an entrepreneur.

Now you'll know the answers for determining who your target market is, where to find your clients, how to open a sales conversation authentically, how to make a sale without feeling pushy or getting rejected, and best of all, you'll receive a blueprint for building a profitable business and increasing your income. Finally, you'll be provided viable strategies for what to do with the massive amount of money you'll soon be earning. You probably haven't even thought that far ahead yet, but you will need to know how to live with your success, once you know exactly how to win.

Regardless of our age or gender, we all need to be at peace financially. We all need to pay our bills, take care of our families, and save for our futures, and there's nothing we want more than to take control of our own lives.

While standing in front of that dumpster, I vowed it was time to take control of my life. I'd had enough and there was no way I was going to dive into that big, green monster. After making that final decision, I went on to bootstrap my own nationwide California C Corporation—Signing Pro, Inc.—from zero to multi-millions, with 23,000 people working under me.

For seventeen years, I was a CEO who walked with giants such as Wells Fargo, Bank of America, Fidelity Title, Lending Tree, prestigious law firms, mortgage brokers, and so many more. Signing Pro, Inc. was the second-largest notary document-signing service in the nation. Perhaps one of my agents came to your home or business to assist you in signing your home purchase, refinance, or sales documents.

In October, 2010, due to a decline in business from the 2007-2008 market debacle, I closed Signing Pro's doors and went on to become one of only 253 CFE Certified Financial Educators® in the United States who speaks on the importance of understanding easy financial principles.

In 2016, I produced and was the host of the show *Maximize Your Wealth Now* (WMAX.TV). This two-season program was designed to enhance financial knowledge globally in an effort to lift public awareness and the economy. You can view all twenty-six episodes on my website at http://maximizeyourwealthnow.com/wmaxtv/.

I am currently a syndicated radio show host, author, international keynote speaker, and the publisher of *Wealthy Woman Magazine.* I am also the owner of Massive Visibility Media™, which specializes in educating coaches, trainers, and entrepreneurs on the answers for transforming their businesses by selling with heart, developing confidence, creating correctly priced saleable programs, and stepping onto stages, web TV, podcasts, and radio for massive marketing visibility.

Believe me, I don't have all of the answers. I'm on this journey called life just like you are, and every day, I enjoy having an opportunity to learn something new from my students. However, I have built multi-million-dollar businesses, so I know how to get you where you want to go. It's not magic. It's simply a step-by-step system that is broken down into small, manageable pieces.

I understand your frustration, and I know you're doing the best you can with what you know in this moment. I want you to know it is okay and I believe in you. Where you are today, with your business, is simply a reflection of what you have or haven't been taught, and when the money gets tight, who can afford to pay $30,000 to get the answers for how to build a successful business?

However, I also believe everyone needs an education in order to move forward in business, so you should make smart decisions about whom you hire.

You've found me now. As you read, let me be your mentor, your coach, your accountability partner, and a shoulder to lean on. Feel free to make notes, highlight, and bend down this book's pages. This is your book, your business bible. It's up to you to decide whether it's going to stay tucked away on your bookshelf or remain at the top of your stack as a reference and guide to overcoming your challenges and creating your business success. You may also want to find a journal to write in any additional thoughts you have beyond the exercises I offer throughout.

The big question is: Are you ready to maximize your wealth now and make a change in your lifestyle? If so, you will need to expand your comfort zone and build your confidence muscles to achieve financial freedom.

Do you want to make a difference in the world by becoming massively visible for massive income? If so, good! Let's get started and take this journey together! Now is your time!

Let's go!

PART ONE
REVEALING THE 3 Cs

"You are essentially who you create yourself to be and all that occurs in your life is the result of your own making."

— Stephen Richards

♡

CHAPTER 1

Diving or Ditching

The most painful point in my dumpster-diving tale is that I went from outrageously wealthy to seriously considering crawling into that dirty, stinky thing just to grab one over-ripe watermelon we probably couldn't possibly eat. The whole idea was a perfect representation of my thinking at that time.

My brain was mush, just like the red pulp oozing inside the green-and-white rind. Have you ever felt that kind of fear, the kind of fear that causes a whirling in your brain so loud you can't think straight?

As my children and I continued to digest the calamity of destitute and broken humans scrambling in and out of the gigantic green container, with overripe melons tucked under their arms, I found myself wondering, *Why can't just one person get into the dumpster and hand each of us a watermelon? Why do all of these poor people, waiting their turn, have to scale the walls?*

The operative word was definitely "poor." My sons and I felt sorry for them. We felt sorry that they had such a challenge getting in and out of the dumpster, and we felt sorry for them because they looked like ragamuffins who'd been living under a bridge half a mile down the road. Unfortunately, I believe their being "poor" resulted from them not knowing the tools that would permit them to work together or the belief that they could change their lifestyles.

THINKING IS BELIEVING

Over my lifetime, I've gained and lost a fortune three times, and each loss was the final result of a marriage gone wrong. These were my biggest financial mistakes and my most expensive golden lessons.

But how could I have forecast that husband number one would be controlling and abusive, number two would be a thief and philanderer, and number three would be a bipolar alcoholic? The reality is no one could have. But here is where the choice of pain or peace provides an opportunity to choose correctly.

With each of these men, I had built powerful, income-generating businesses. Each divorce presented a golden lesson that forced me to choose between wallowing in my pain and misfortune or learning from my mistakes, joyfully accepting peace, and embarking on a greatly appreciated do-over.

Without these unfortunate lessons, I wouldn't be where I am today, and I most definitely wouldn't be who I am: a strong, independent businesswoman who leads with love and builds vast worldwide communities with heart.

Standing at the dumpster, I suddenly realized you always have a choice, and it's what you choose to think, speak, and believe that makes all the difference in your future. If you were standing there, with your two small children, what would you have chosen pain or peace? Would you have chosen to dive into the dumpster or ditched the whole idea?

Suddenly, my five-year-old looked up at me, with the wisdom of an old soul, stating clearly the words I'd already decided to act on: "Let's go home, Mommy. The rice and beans are fine with me. I don't need a watermelon." We had both chosen peace.

Since that time, I think carefully before making decisions. I take the time to sit quietly and evaluate those decisions' long-term effects on my life and how they will affect those who surround me. In every case, I choose to take the high road toward peace.

Later that day, while the boys played blissfully on the beach, I sat at the tiny trailer table, writing a three-step strategy that would change my life, maximize my wealth, and most importantly, guarantee I would never be required to consider dumpster-diving again.

WORKING WITH UNIVERSAL FLOW

It's a known universal principle that you are meant to be happy here in Earth School and receive all you desire. But wouldn't you agree that sometimes it doesn't feel that way? I believe the trials you go through are lessons you failed to learn, presented once again.

Where you made a faulty choice or misstep, you can make a better decision next time and escape the pain. But when opportunity presents itself, you have to make the choice to see your part in it, change the way you look at the challenge, and then choose the right steps into peace. The question is: Are you awake enough to see your opportunities and the options of peace on your path?

It's when you talk about your mistakes over and over and over again that you bring more pain into your life. This behavior literally tells the Universe you want more pain. Talking negatively to anyone who is within earshot, thinking angry thoughts, and blaming others tells the Universe you want more of the same, and so you get more pain.

Each time a golden lesson is presented, you are forced to decide whether now is the time for your wake-up call or whether you will continue to wallow in your anger as a victim. Before you decide, the wise action is to take the time to quiet your mind and examine closely your misfortune. This examination will enable you to change your ways and create a positive outcome.

The Buddha made it known that "What you have become is what you have thought." This is also known as the Law of Attraction. Simply put, the Law of Attraction is the ability to attract into your life whatever you are focusing on. The Law of Attraction uses the power of the mind to translate whatever is in your thoughts and materializes them into reality.

In basic terms, all thoughts eventually turn into things. If you focus on doom and gloom, you will remain under the darkness of that cloud. If you focus on positive thoughts and have goals you aim to achieve, you will find a way to achieve them with massive action and support from the Universe.

The Law of Attraction is considered to be one of life's biggest mysteries, and very few people are fully aware of how much of an influence it has on their day-to-day lives. Whether you are doing it knowingly or unknowingly, every second of your existence, you are acting as a human magnet, sending out your thoughts and emotions and attracting back to you more of what you put out.

Sending out the wrong thoughts and attracting more unwanted emotions and events into your life is why you may not be living the lifestyle you deserve. Having said this, discovering the Law of Attraction is at work within your life should be a great cause for celebration! Once you clearly understand the power of the Law of Attraction and you have mastered how to apply it effectively in your everyday life, your entire future is yours to create.

PENNING THE 3 Cs: CLEARING—CLARITY—CONFIDENCE

In the quiet of my little trailer, I stopped to breathe, reflect, and focus on how I had gotten to this place in my life. How could I go from vastly rich to penniless in what seemed like overnight? I had made many, many, many golden mistakes to learn from, but I had very little knowledge about how to correct the desperate situation we were living in. That was when the theory of the life-changing 3 Cs led me to financial freedom and wealth.

As I closed my eyes, I could hear the waves crashing against the shore, the seagulls calling as they flew overhead, and the voices of my darling children bantering back and forth while building sand-castles. *How fortunate I am to be alive, healthy, and at peace in this moment*, I thought. I learned at a very young age that no matter how life challenged me, there was always something to be grateful for. And so I began to write.

The 3 Cs—clearing, clarity, and confidence—were delivered into my mind faster than I could pen them on the yellow pad. Writing while meditating is a practiced art that I picked up at the age of sixteen, and I still use it to this day. Later, reviewing words that seemed more like they were channeled to me than they were my own, I vowed to act on them diligently, knowing there would soon be a shift that would take the three of us to a better lifestyle.

Following the step-by-step system of the 3 Cs changed my life and my income; it brought loving and caring friends into my world, and it surrounded me with a beautiful community of entrepreneurs. If this is a snapshot of the life you wish to live, get out a pen and feel free to make this book your own while learning how to Sell Through Your Heart.

Let's look at each of the 3 Cs in detail. Each one is a step that builds upon the next.

STEP 1: CLEARING—YOUR STEPPING STONES TO SUCCESS

Clearing your past creates clarity about the lessons learned from the mistakes you've attracted. I say "mistakes you've attracted" because you can't blame anyone else but yourself. We all look at the same problem or challenge differently, but it's how you choose to think about the other person or problem that creates pain and loss in your life. It's simply your perception of what is, and you have the power to change that perception anytime you wish.

Ask yourself these questions and check off the statements that relate to your behaviors:

Is This You?

☐ Do you always have to be right?

☐ Are you walking over another person's boundaries without thinking about his or her feelings?

☐ Is it your practice to think and talk about only you, you, you?

☐ Do you anger easily and take control of every decision, making others feel as if they must walk on eggshells to keep the peace?

☐ Are you a liar, telling stories that aren't true except in your own mind?

☐ Have you been critical and judgmental while hurting another's feelings?

☐ Is it your nature to blame everyone else but yourself?

☐ Are you a downer, thinking only negative thoughts and whining to anyone who will listen?

☐ Do you harbor resentments and hate toward others and cast them out of your life?

☐ Have you abused, lashed out, or physically hurt those closest to you?

☐ Is it your selfish way or the highway?

☐ Have you stolen the attention in another's moment of glory?

☐ Are you addicted to alcohol and/or drugs while saying you're fine and that you've got it all under control?

How many on this list do you identify with? Who are you hurting? Why are you lashing out and causing pain for yourself and others?

If you are seeing and experiencing lots of challenges that cause you pain, honey, it's you. You are the one ingredient that is always the same in the mix, and it's you that has the power to fix and change it. If you choose not to change your ways, the Universe won't be open to creating a better life for you.

When It's Not Your Fault

On the other hand, if someone else made the choice to hurt you and you didn't retaliate or create that person's pain, it's not your problem and you're not required to take responsibility for his or her actions. It's a challenge within that person.

I know of a mom who has a son she loves dearly. Twenty years ago, he cast her out of his life and chose to take on his father's anger, hate, and vengeance as a result of a divorce that occurred over twenty-two years before. Even though his father and his mom have made amends and worked things out, this forty-year-old child continues the battle with his mom in his own mind. To this day, he refuses to speak to her even while passing in a narrow stairway. The mom has chosen to create peace in her mind while giving him some space to work through his personal pain.

The purpose of sharing this story is to let you know some relationships may have no hope of healing because the problem is within the mind of another and nothing can be done until that person sees clearly the pain was not created by you. The illness resides in his thinking and only he can resolve and release his pain. There is no repercussion for you in letting it go and giving another soul time to heal.

Seeing Into Your Mirrors

In his interview with me on WMAX.TV, bestselling author and human behavior expert Dr. John Demartini said, "Every relationship is really part of the perfection. It's giving you feedback to let you know what you haven't loved in yourself and yet you're projecting it onto other people."

Think about what challenges and relationship problems may be going on around you. This morning, I woke to my neighbors screaming at each other—I have no idea about what. I do know, however, that one of my neighbor ladies creates conflict with everyone and blames the other person. She can't see that the one major factor in every conflict is that she is smack-dab in the middle of it.

At times when I've chatted with her about these outbursts, she expresses to me that in these situations, she feels like she's being attacked. She then becomes angry, stirring up a storm of hateful comments and criticism about whomever she perceives to be wrong. In every situation, regardless of whether the other person was right or wrong, she is the problem because it's her thinking that causes her pain.

We all experience this type of challenge, but it's how we choose to think and talk about it that makes all the difference. Think about and write in detail your most recent difficulty. Be really honest with yourself. If you were a witness standing idly by, what would it look like? Can you see yourself as part of the problem? Write down how this challenge occurred, what you think went wrong, and how you participated in the escalation.

_____

_____

_____

_____

_____

_____

How can you expect to turn around a miserable situation if you aren't honest with both yourself and the other person involved? Denying how bad a situation is only digs you into a deeper hole.

Those closest to you are mirrors of what you will most likely see inside yourself if you aren't afraid to take the time to reflect. When someone consistently irritates and aggravates you, it's because you have that same behavior within you. Close your eyes for a minute and think of someone who irritates you. What irritates you most about this person? Now take the next step and look within yourself. Are you exhibiting those same behaviors unconsciously? If you weren't, you wouldn't be irritated. In fact, you wouldn't see it at all. It's just that simple.

Seeing the errors within allows you to forgive yourself and the others involved. The action of forgiving yourself provides an opportunity to see your part in the pain and creates the space to move forward with confidence, knowing you won't have to learn that lesson again. That doesn't mean you won't be tested again with a similar challenge. Believe me; you will be tested again just to see whether you got it right.

Don't take yourself so seriously. We all stumble and fall. At times, we even make fools of ourselves. Instead of getting frustrated and freaked out like my neighbor, try smiling so you can move on. It's so much more productive for your mental, emotional, and physical wellbeing.

Revealing Your Golden Stepping Stones

Remembering that mistakes are your stepping-stones to success, I believe there really are no mistakes because you don't know what you don't know. You only do the best you can, in that moment, with the knowledge you have already learned or been taught.

Most of us have challenges that repeat over and over again. The people involved may change, but the basis of the problem does not. These incidents are meant to teach us lessons that we may not clearly see the first, second, or third time, and they always begin with the same feelings of pain and end with a negative result.

In the lines below, write out your challenging incident, but give yourself the space and time to see the error in how you perceive each of these repeated difficulties. Think about your deepest thoughts, what you might have said that you knew would cut painfully through the other person, and evaluate the actions that caused the problem to ratchet into a higher level of anger, a lack of communication, and in some cases, alienation.

Ask yourself…

Whom did I hurt?

_____

_____

What was I thinking?

_____

_____

_____

What actions did I take?

_____

_____

_____

Clearing Negative Thoughts for Positive Incomes

The art of clearing negative thoughts and behaviors begins with taking a bit of time to look inward through small moments of meditation. I can hear you already: "I can't meditate. I've tried that already. It doesn't work for me." If this is what you tell yourself, it is what you will receive. Henry Ford said, "Whether you think you can or you think you can't, you're right." Remember, the Universe wants to make you happy, so when you say, "I can't" to yourself, it's exactly what you receive.

Let's try something different. My dear friend Sterling Sumaya O'Grady says, "Yes, you can meditate. It's in your genes." So maybe it's time to pull on your big-kid pants and change the way you think about this very important step in your evolution and business success.

Together, we're trying to turn a big ship that's been traveling in a negative direction around into a positive direction, which will ultimately enable you to receive and live the lifestyle you deserve.

If you've been on a cruise ship, you know how long it takes the captain to make this massive turn. Imagine how much preparation, time, patience, and education it took to accomplish this goal. Without the required study, the captain might take out the whole pier before turning the ship's bow out to sea. Wouldn't you suppose he performed this same task at least 1,000 times in a simulator before being trusted to grasp the wheel?

Now is your opportunity to practice turning the ship of your life around simply by quieting your mind and simulating the changes necessary to correct and overcome your personal challenges. This valuable time allows you to look at your participation and clear your thinking in a way that brings positive outcomes.

Preparing for Peace

Preparing a place to meditate is important if you want to achieve successful results. Make sure you will be undisturbed for at least five to thirty minutes. Meditation lengths vary, but they are rarely more than thirty minutes in duration. Sitting up is best. In the beginning, you'll likely fall asleep, and that's okay. At least you made the effort to stop the mind chatter and connect with a new way of thinking.

Pick a chair, mat, or a zafu (round meditation cushion) that will be comfortable for you. Sit in an erect, upright position that you can stay relaxed in. Close your eyes or focus on a lit candle. If you are outside, look out into space through the leaves of a tree.

It might be useful to stretch before settling in, even if only for a few minutes. Yoga poses or any other stretching exercises are fine; they help relax the body and allow for more energy flow. After your meditation is over, a stretch for integration is also useful.

Don't be surprised if you begin to feel unusual physical sensations like tingling, numbness, heaviness, heat, floating, or heightened senses. You may also feel restlessness or itching. These phenomena will subside as you deepen your ability to meditate and the body becomes more accustomed to holding these energies.

Feel free to meditate as often as you wish. If you feel resistance, or if things start changing too fast for you, take a break from the meditations for a while. Follow your intuition. The number of meditations you choose to do in a week is your decision. It all depends on how quickly you want to move through your clearing exercises. For many, once a day is fine. I prefer the early morning because it's quiet with few disturbances. Develop a consistent routine, at about the same time of day, so your body becomes accustomed to the meditative exercise.

Try not to have expectations about your meditations. Write down the challenge you are experiencing and ask for support before you begin. Let whatever unfolds be the right experience for you. Each time you meditate, it will be a different experience. One time you might have a wonderful experience, and the next day, a so-so experience. Don't be discouraged if this happens.

The path of meditation holds many lessons, and one of the lessons is to be unattached to having a perfect experience every time you sit in meditation. Don't try to recreate the same meditation by referring to a memory of your previous experiences. Let it be different each time and a fresh, new experience. Try not to make something happen; just let it unfold and stay relaxed.

If thoughts keep popping into your mind, an easy way to regain focus is by focusing on your breath while counting in rhythms of four. Learn from your ordinary meditations as well as your exhilarating ones.

Journaling Your Progress

Keep a pen and your journal nearby so you can write down revelations about your life, yourself, what distracting thoughts or feelings came up, and how to quiet them. Write any insights, ideas, messages, or epiphanies you receive. If people come up in your mind, send light and love to them and continue what you were doing. When someone pops up in your meditation, he or she is usually asking for support, love, or acknowledgment from you on some level or another.

If you are sleepy or have just eaten, do your meditation at another time. If, in the meditation, you are unable to follow the directions or feel as if you are rocking or floating, be at ease with this feeling and let go. Don't come out of a floaty state because it will lead to a deeper meditation experience. Normally, you can catch the phrases in your thoughts during the meditation that are important for you to hear.

Sometimes you might forget what happened completely. You know you were meditating and things were happening, but your conscious mind might have difficulty remembering. You use the same faculties for dream recall as you do for meditation recall. As you develop the ability to translate your otherworldly experiences in conscious thought, this problem will dissipate. Just keep practicing your meditations and your recall abilities will improve.

Sitting upright during your meditation will enable you to straddle the sleep-awake border more easily. The goal of meditation is to gain the ability to straddle the sleep-awake border with full consciousness intact. This is where the "sweet spot" is—the doorway to the worlds within you, and the deep stillness that is sought by spiritual candidates and teachers.

Let whatever happens in your meditation be the right experience for you on that day; it may be quite different the next time. There is no wrong way to experience a meditation. These are subjective experiences that are unique to every individual, and they vary in states of consciousness.

What are the five biggest mistakes relative to the behaviors you checked off in the *Is This You?* list earlier in this chapter? These mistakes might include arguments with your spouse or family members, people you've cast out of your life, misunderstandings with parents, divorces, money challenges, or screaming hateful words directed at your roommate.

Meeting Yourself Head-On

You've already determined what challenge has been repeating itself, evaluated what happened, and determined what your part was in the process. Now it's time to answer the six most important questions regarding the five people you've hurt in the past.

Write out the answers to the following six questions for each of your five personal challenges (They can be past experiences you've chosen to bury or current issues you are dealing with.):

1. Who am I angry, disappointed, or annoyed with, sad about, or over-the-top pissed at?

    _____

    _____

    _____

2. What is this challenge about and how did it get that way?

    _____

    _____

    _____

3. How did I contribute to it? What was my part?

_____

_____

_____

4. When in my history did this same type of problem happen before?

_____

_____

_____

5. How could I look at this challenge as a witness standing by?

_____

_____

_____

6. What was my golden learning experience?

_____

_____

_____

If you feel complete, forgive yourself and those you hurt. Then let it go and chalk it up as a golden learning experience you never intend to repeat.

If you aren't able to reach closure with questions 2, 4, and 5, give it time. Keep working at it. The answers will come, and once they do, you'll be released to move toward your next steps in growth. Practice looking within until the things you look at change.

STEP 2: CLARITY—BREAKING THROUGH CONFUSION

Once you've completed the clearing process and revealed the truth to yourself, clarity becomes your new best friend. Step 2 involves breaking through confusion into clarity. Once it becomes clear your mistakes are simply golden lessons you're meant to learn in Earth School, the confusion and pain begin to subside, and you realize all of your struggles coincide with the Law of Attraction.

When I was standing in front of that dumpster, my confusion drifted away and my clarity of perspective was that I had no intention of being poor. In fact, that thought was so foreign to me I couldn't even form the word poor because, in reality, I was especially wealthy in knowledge. Fortunately, another golden tool in my toolbox had strengthened my foundation and would serve to maximize my wealth.

STEP 3: CONFIDENCE—IMPLEMENTING MASSIVE VISIBILITY

Once you have a solid foundation, a business blueprint, and a system for sales in place, they will boost your confidence. Confidence is the third C. With confidence, you can do anything you set your mind to. Absolutely nothing is out of reach except for quieting your little mind that doesn't yet believe you. That's what meditation is for.

Confidence says you are not your thoughts unless you let them take control. Even fear isn't a match for confidence because fear is simply a state of mind that can be changed.

About fear, the yogi mystic Sadhguru says:

> Fear is simply because you are not living with life; you are living in your mind. Your fear is always about what's going to happen next. That means your fear is always about that which does not exist. If your fear is about the non-existent, your fear is one hundred percent imaginary.

If you look at fear carefully, what is it really? Have you noticed your fear is never about what happened in the past? It is always about what might happen in the future. The future hasn't happened yet. It doesn't even exist. Being fearful of a future that doesn't exist doesn't make sense.

Millions of people are living in the future and that's why they experience fear. The only thing you can do about fear is to get real, notice your thoughts, stop living in the future, and start focusing on living in the now or you'll miss it.

Sure, I could have freaked out and decided I might end up under a bridge, like the ragamuffins taking the dive for watermelons, but I decided to live for only that day and let the Universe take care of tomorrow because I knew what I believed I would most assuredly receive.

It's important to learn a new way of responding to your old way of thinking. Focus on what is right now and avoid imagining a possibility that doesn't exist. When you're feeling confident, it's easier to resist any fearful thought. In this way, you can begin to manipulate and bring peace into how life revolves around you. When you choose not to let fear control your mind, your confidence will soar, enabling you to step into community leadership, massive visibility, and multiple streams of income.

Creating massive visibility through confidence includes speaking on stages, knowing how to present yourself in a way that makes show hosts shine, speaking in three-minute sound bites, and showing up professionally for video, web TV, and Zoom interviews. You know how to do two-minute videos your clients are waiting to watch, and you are prepared to step into the light to present yourself and your business in a way that calls others to you while creating a massive income.

REACHING FOR THE ULTIMATE GOAL

You are now in possession of the magic formula of the 3 Cs. Since it's such a big part of your business foundation, I ask that you not ignore or jump over the importance of each step in this process.

You always have free will, but discounting or overlooking a step will severely delay your progress. It's a daily practice, and you'll find over time that more and more stuff will surface to be reckoned with. Take your time and continue your practice until all of your past infractions have been evaluated, forgiven, and cleared.

The ultimate goal of the 3 Cs is to get people talking about how much they love you. The rules for accomplishing this goal are to say nothing unkind about anyone, give of your time and knowledge from the deepest recesses of your heart, and understand what you give to another may not be returned by the same person, but it will most assuredly come back to you in other unexpected, positive ways.

Remember, the 3 Cs are a part of your foundation, and by using them, you'll continue to grow, thrive, and, finally, become part of the 20 percent of entrepreneurs who become successful in a viable, income-generating business.

"Our very survival depends on our ability to stay awake, to adjust to new ideas, to remain vigilant, and to face the challenge of change."

— Rev. Dr. Martin Luther King, Jr.

♡

CHAPTER 2

Designing Your Business Blueprint

Now that you've put the 3 Cs into practice and discovered the secrets for steering your ship into positive waters, without wiping out the pier, it's time to elaborate on what it means to be an entrepreneur mastering the art of creating a winning business.

In this chapter, we'll discuss what it means to compel your clients to work with you instead of working with old, pushy sales techniques that chase your clients away. We'll talk about the two personality types in Earth School and how they interact in the business world. I'll show you how to design and set up your business blueprint. Finally, we have an agreement to make that we'll get to later.

According to the financial analyst company Bloomberg, eight out of ten entrepreneurs who start businesses fail within the first eighteen months. A whopping 80 percent crash and burn. But why? And what can we learn from the colossal failures of so many small businesses that we can apply to our own business aspirations?

In my thirty-plus years as a solopreneur, and through my interactions with thousands of entrepreneurs around the globe via my company, Maximize Your Wealth Now, I have had an opportunity to watch the confusion and pain business owners experience as they take on the challenges of being an entrepreneur alone. They become confused by so many different opinions of what they should do, distracted by shiny new ideas and overwhelmed by big visions, with no step-by-step instructions. Many don't understand the importance of deciding on a specific target market, how to find one, and what to say to create sales and generate an income.

On the surface, Bloomberg reports that the primary reason so many businesses fail is because they simply run out of cash. However, the cracks in their foundations start well before their financial collapses.

SEVEN REASONS SOLOPRENEURS FAIL

Reason 1: No finely defined target market

Reason 2: No understanding of how the client thinks or what his or her needs are

Reason 3: No clarity on how to build client relationships

Reason 4: No authentic, heartfelt sales skills

Reason 5: No confidence in program development or pricing

Reason 6: No visibility in the marketplace or on the web

Reason 7: No video or blog branding consistency

Your customers hold the keys to your success in their pain, behavior, confusion, core values, and the dreams they want to fulfill, experience, feel, and enjoy.

The information I'm about to share comes from more than twenty-eight years of trial and error, testing, experimenting, and tweaking the refined answers to overcoming solopreneur failures. In the business world, we call this "focusing on the end result."

CHASING THE BUSINESS

Becoming an entrepreneur, running a business, marketing, and generating sales all at the same time is like playing in a one-man band. Unfortunately, most of us aren't taught the "how tos" of running a business during our educational years. In fact, we're all taught to be good employees and pay our taxes to keep the economy going. As an employee, you're in the highest tax bracket, so why would the government provide an education on how to become an entrepreneur with massive amounts of tax write-offs? That's not how the rules of our system work.

Having a business means you have literally chosen to participate in the School of Hard Knocks while learning the success formulas of an entrepreneur. In this class, you can expect to make lots of mistakes before reaching your intended goal and waving the gold flag of financial freedom. Be aware that what you'll experience, during your growth, may be laborious, time-consuming, and expensive, but it will all be worth it if you stay focused on the end results of thriving success and financial freedom.

CHARTING YOUR JOURNEY

Tacking is a practice that moves you through many failures and mistakes while believing those mistakes are only your growing and stretching experiences. It's also a test to see whether you'll give up easily and say, "Oh, that doesn't work." Or push forward saying,

"Well, that didn't work for me. I see that I did it wrong and I'll fix it next time I get a new opportunity to try again. Next!"

Those who have been in business for ten years or more understand the meaning of their mistakes and build on them to achieve a successful outcome. Captains and sailors talk about tacking back and forth to reach their chosen destinations. They know that if their navigation is off by even one-tenth of an inch at the start, they'll be miles away from their intended destination at the end of their journeys. A good captain charts a journey and tacks back and forth, correcting small and, sometimes, massive mistakes. In every correction, he learns what doesn't work and focuses on what does in an effort to become successful. A promising entrepreneur will take the same journey by first creating a business blueprint and then sticking to it while making small, significant corrections that support each step forward.

The trick is to stay focused on your business blueprint and avoid becoming distracted by the many bright, shiny objects thought to be a great idea at the time that cause deviations from your plan. This habit of distraction creates unnecessary losses of time and frequently causes expenditures that deplete your bank account and cause unnecessary burnout and fear.

ALIGNING RIGHT INTENTION WITH YOUR MISSION

Ask yourself whether your intention aligns with your mission. Does it match your values and your passion? How do you wish to be of service?

Webster defines intention as "a determination to act in a particular way to do or achieve an aim or purpose." Intention is an extremely important consideration when developing your business blueprint and determining your course of direction to reach your end result. Ask yourself first, "What is my motive and purpose for planning, marketing, and selling this idea or line of products? How does it relate to my back-story experience, training, and certifications?"

Some believe their intention is the same as their passion, but these words have two entirely different meanings. Your passions are your emotions, your intensity, and the driving force for mastering your business' success. Your passion is what keeps you focused on your desired interest and end result.

Your intention is to develop a business that will support others and make you money so you have the ability to give freely to others. However, if you are not passionate about what your business represents, it will be extremely difficult to maintain it as part of your life.

Some entrepreneurs believe they were given their passion prior to arriving here on Earth, and if they could just figure out what it is, they'd know exactly what to do as a business. But this is not necessarily true. Your passion is all about what you love to do, and your intention is the way in which you choose to do it. You can be passionate about anything that excites you enough to roll out of bed at 4:30 a.m., get to work, and accomplish your next goal. Your passion is not something you have to know or find in order to do your business.

GROWING THROUGH STRUGGLE

Many entrepreneurs dream big, but they do little, if anything, to realize their dreams. Then there are those who are able to transform their dreams into a massive income.

Did you know that strength grows out of resistance? Our characters and successes as solopreneurs are built on setbacks, learning experiences, temporary defeat, and lots of golden mistakes. Strength and growth come only through continuous effort and struggle. I believe our biggest enemy to combat is right between our ears. You cannot fail if you keep moving forward while making small changes in your business blueprint that make big differences in your end results.

Edison understood this principle and attempted to light our future 1,000 times before succeeding in inventing the electric light bulb. Colonel Sanders went to 1,000 restaurant owners hoping to sell his little chicken recipe. In the process, he made 1,000 sales pitches, 999 mistakes, and 999 corrections until he got it right. Because of his persistence and the slight course corrections in his sales pitch, he not only sold his recipe, but he made billions of dollars selling chicken.

Any challenge can be overcome with persistence and a willingness to do your best work. The secret is to believe in your heart that you will succeed if shown the perfect step-by-step process to achieve success. But it's not enough to have the steps and do nothing with them. You must be honest with yourself, take action, and never give up, even if you're scared and feel like you're in uncharted waters. You can do this!

THE SECRET TO RECOGNIZING YOUR PROGRESS

Two of the most common mistakes entrepreneurs make are not using a method to track their successes and investing in expensive, long-term programs that go on and on without any definitive breakthrough guidelines.

Because we're all alone in the building of our businesses and others don't recognize the milestones of success we achieve, we don't see them. Worse still, there's no baseline set, so it's difficult to see any visible signs of progress.

This is exactly why I suggest a business blueprint be written prior to beginning your journey. This way you are able to check off the steps as you move through and accomplish each task, giving you a feeling of "atta-girl" or "atta-boy" and getting a high-five when you've reached your intended goal. If you're a High C, you get to check the boxes off as you go down a detailed list. Woo-hoo! (We'll talk more about High Cs in Chapter 6.)

I set definitive goals for myself and tell everyone in my inner circle about them. That way, my community holds me accountable. My inner circle receives frequent text updates from me as I move through the tasks, and we all celebrate together when I accomplish my intended goal. In my courses, each of my students practices this same process and appreciates the support of community and rewarded celebration.

A good example of this system of reward was utilized while creating this book. Everyone in my inner circle was well aware I was required to reach between 50,000 and 60,000 words, so I kept track of how many words I'd written and sent out text messages with my progress. My Massive Visibility Entrepreneurs community members would, in turn, text me with a thumbs up or an encouraging comment. This kept me going and kept them in the loop (remember: people are watching), and when the book sailed off to the editor, we were all relieved together and celebrating my achievement.

This same rewards system works for my students during my courses. Students are given a blueprint of what is included in the course. Each week, they receive homework assignments and report back with the results, giving them a secure feeling of having accomplished their goals. When they reach their intended destinations, we celebrate together. This allows them to build confidence and feel they succeeded in overcoming and completing the next big hurdle.

LEARNING AS YOU GO

Before beginning your blueprint, know that nothing is perfect. Don't be concerned about the tiniest details; you can fill those in as you move along. If it has to be perfect, you'll create delays and anxiety in your progress. This is not the time to be nit-picky.

Keep in mind your clients really don't care about how perfect your blueprint is. That's only for you. They are ordinary people who want you to be authentically you. Being a perfectionist at this stage will hold you back unnecessarily until everything is just so. If I'd done that with this book, you never would have been able to receive the benefit of the information I intended to provide for your business.

The same goes for you. Your people are waiting for you, so don't be a stickler with the details. Let's call this a rough draft. Nothing is cut in stone and everything can be massaged and changed at a later date. Just get something down on paper.

WRITING YOUR BUSINESS BLUEPRINT

Go to ShirleneReeves.com to download your Free Blueprint Checklist so you can follow along and check off each task upon completion. You'll find it by clicking on the Resources button and selecting the Free Stuff page.

I liken your business to a lighthouse. I'm so happy when I visit my home on the beach in San Felipe, Baja California, Mexico, because I can see our beautiful lighthouse from the big bay windows in my living room. The lighthouse sits out by the Gulf of California (a.k.a. the Sea of Cortés) and glistens in rich, deep colors of blue, turquoise, or purple. A beautiful backdrop of mountains, called the "Rockadile," due to its unique shape, frames it.

First thing every morning, I relax into a comfy chair on my deck while sipping a cup of steamy, hot coffee, and then I gaze at the strength and stability of the lighthouse, standing white and tall in the glistening sunlight. It's anchored onto the cliff in a foundation of rebar and cement. It's not on shifting sands, so I know it's always going to be there.

At night, I can see only a silhouette of the lighthouse, but its beam still shines brightly, waiting to guide ship captains into the Bay of San Felipe. The point here is when you develop a blueprint that creates a strong, solid foundation, you will always be standing in a place where your clients can find you.

STEPPING OUT OF THE HOBBY ZONE

Over the years, interacting with business owners, I've heard all kinds of stories about how they started their business hobby. I say "hobby" because you don't have a business until you are making a consistent income.

Entrepreneurs start their businesses for so many good reasons: maybe they had an experience in life they think others should be aware of, maybe they've always dreamed of owning their own business and becoming their own boss, or they write a book and finally decide to become an entrepreneur. The reasons are vast and many, but few really understand what they're getting into and quickly become overwhelmed.

I continually observe entrepreneurs who are completely lost and confused about how to build a business because they don't know how to evolve out of the hobby zone into a full-fledged, income-generating business. The key to this evolution is a simple step-by-step plan using a simple business blueprint as their guide, designed specifically for their field of expertise.

Instead of sitting down and writing out a plan, speaking to someone who can assist in developing their plan, or hiring a coach who will save them time and money, many small business owners leap into ordering business cards, selecting branding colors, setting up a website, attending marketing and networking events, and then attach a name to all this activity, saying, "There it is: that's my business."

But their statements are all air and, if you take a moment to begin questioning what they're selling and whom they're selling it to, you can see the anxiety rush up from within their core because there's nothing behind their unstructured sales pitch. They feel a great deal of fear and anxiety because there's no foundation behind what they're saying to potential clients.

Without a plan to chart your course and a well-developed foundation of programs, these gaping black holes keep entrepreneurs from opening sales conversations or knowing what to say when someone asks what they do. They fumble around with their words and go on laboriously with sentence after sentence, attempting to offer some sort of explanation that makes sense.

PARLAYING INTO A BUSINESS PARTNERSHIP

Here's my favorite scenario about how entrepreneurial businesses get started. You're out partying or sitting at the kitchen table drinking a beer and your friend comes up with what he thinks is a great idea for a business. You blurt out, "Let's do it! That's a great idea and we can be partners!"

Instantly, you are in a partnership, with no written agreement, that almost always ends badly. Word to the wise: Never, ever go into business without a legal agreement or you'll probably lose your drinking buddy. We don't plan to fail. We simply fail to plan.

SYSTEMIZING FOR SUCCESS

Well-meaning entrepreneurs unknowingly practice the habit of putting the cart before the horse. They have no concept of how to market and sell their product or service efficiently, and because they haven't carefully defined who their target market is, they make massive, costly, golden mistakes.

It's important you learn who your target market is, develop and provide programs your clients want and desire, learn how to market and sell to your clients, and then write and sell a book for the purposes of leaving a legacy and acquiring keynote speaking opportunities and massive visibility.

Do not run around looking for people to sell to. Instead, create your foundational blueprint, learn the art of selling with heart, and then build a marketing plan to beam your light brightly so your clients can easily find you. This three-step process keeps you from running aimlessly from one networking group to the next looking for your people.

By the way, have you ever seen a lighthouse running up and down the beach searching for captains? Me neither. Are you running up and down the beach trying to sell your books, products, and services? I did, too, in the beginning. That was one of my golden mistakes, and I hear the same thing from entrepreneurs all over the globe.

"The critical ingredient is getting off your butt and doing something. It's as simple as that. A lot of people have ideas, but there are few who decide to do something about them now. Not tomorrow. Not next week. But today. The true entrepreneur is a doer, not a dreamer."

— Nolan Bushnell, founder of Atari

♡

CHAPTER 3

Developing
A Strong Foundation

We've talked a lot about why you need a business blueprint that will support you in standing firmly on your foundation while beaming your light with massive visibility. In this chapter, you'll learn the answers for how to stop running up and down the beach and start supporting the backbone of your business.

Here's the big secret and your ultimate goal: Instead of running, stand firmly in a place where your clients can find you for support. They need to be able to reach out at any time, make the call, and ask you for support, but if you aren't clear about how to stand there, they can't hear what you're saying and simply won't trust you enough to pay thousands of dollars for your service.

OVERCOMING FEAR THROUGH CLARITY

Begin strengthening your foundation by overcoming your fears with clarity and a positive step-by-step perspective. Soon, a business you can be proud of will begin to swell with momentum and you'll enjoy riding the wave out of the hobby zone toward a substantial income.

Even if you've been in business for eons, treat your next steps like your business is in its infancy because, if you aren't making a consistent income, it truly is. Begin developing your business blueprint by answering the questions below. Think carefully about how you define what you do as a business, its purpose, and your qualifications for providing the product or service your business offers.

Reflect inward, breathe, and write, in detail, the answers to the following three questions.

1. What is the purpose of my business? Describe your intention and purpose without using the word "help." Explain why you are choosing to do this specific business.

    _____

    _____

    _____

    _____

2. What qualifies you to represent this field of expertise? Explain your experience, your credentials, and why you feel you are qualified to do this business.

    _____

    _____

    _____

    _____

3. Describe, in two succinct sentences, what you intend to do that will meet the needs of your clients and provide the benefits that will change their lives.

_____

_____

_____

_____

When you decide to become an entrepreneur, you make a big commitment. Your business is all-encompassing and all-consuming. It becomes your baby, your livelihood, and your new best friend.

If you desire to live an awesome lifestyle, you'll eat, sleep, and breathe your business into life. It literally takes over and, at times, can be a very lonely journey. This is the purpose of knowing your "why." When the going gets tough, a vivid memory of "why" you chose to become an entrepreneur pulls you through.

Let me support you with a few positive reasons for why we, as entrepreneurs, endure the challenges and stick with the process.

BUSINESS BENEFITS

While it may be hard to envision your business taking over your life, understand that it also provides you with many great benefits that you wouldn't have otherwise.

Tax benefits are a biggie and one of the reasons I suggest to entrepreneurs that they do their best to create a business and keep it going.

A business provides a lot of "write-offs" when you are making money. I'm not an accountant, so it's not my place to go deeply into the tax benefits and laws. However, I can provide you with the system I use personally that kept me squeaky-clean during the last three-year audit. The IRS walked away with nothing, but my accountant and my assistant charged me $2,500 for their services. That was a small fee compared to the $30,000 the IRS claimed I owed and, besides, I can add this cost to the legal and accounting column and write it off.

SYSTEMIZING RECEIPTS

It's important to keep a checking and credit card account specifically for your business. Do not pay for some things out of a personal account and others out of your business account. If you do pay for something personal with your business account, be sure to write yourself a check to reimburse the business account. Keep it clean.

The purpose of this important step is to keep your business and you, as an individual, separate in the eyes of the IRS. Then, if an audit should come up for your business, it can't go into your personal accounts and vice versa.

Receipts: Be sure to keep your receipts. I keep a small, brown envelope in my car and put every receipt in it for a month. My next step is to forward the envelope to my assistant, who matches my receipts to my business credit card statements while categorizing my expenses. This system makes it easy for tracking purposes and your bookkeeper will love you for it. You'll be happy, too, when you do your taxes because you'll have many more write-offs than you thought, and you won't need to spend valuable time assembling your receipts at the end of the year.

Meals with clients: Keep your receipts and write the name of the person you had the meal with on the back of the receipt. Use your business credit card and add the receipt to your envelope.

Travel: Wow, do I love to travel! And traveling for business is even better. You can write off your airline tickets, car rentals, meals, and hotel expenses. What more could you ask?

Events: If you are putting on an event or attending an event and providing food or purchasing food there, you can write that off, too.

Gifts: When I travel, I love to buy gifts for my clients. If you choose to buy a gift for your client, be sure to write his or her name on the back of the receipt.

Office and field supplies: The cell phone and its monthly bills, printers, paper and ink, your desk, a new printer, and anything you need for your business is all a write-off. If you need a new computer, be sure to buy it before the end of the year so you can use it as a write-off in that year.

Office Space: Write off your office space at home. Measure the area you use for your office and give the measurements to your accountant. Your accountant will then calculate the percentage of your use based on the size of your home and apply that percentage to a year of your mortgage/rental and utility payments as a write-off in that year. You cannot write off a bedroom with a bed in it, but you can add a hide-a-bed and use it as a couch for your office. (Note: Some accountants won't write off office space in the home. If they won't, then don't hire them.)

Cars: If you lease your car, you can write off your payments 100 percent. If you choose to own your car, ask your accountant for the best option.

Keep in mind that, no matter what you do, you must have the invoices, statements, and receipts to back up your claims. That's why it's great to have a good bookkeeper on your advisory team.

REVEALING YOUR FIVE RICHEST VALUES

Before selecting your advisory team, list your values and get your team onboard with your values so they'll know where they stand and how you expect business to be conducted. Your values are the core of your business and the basis for how you intend to serve your clients. They are the cohesive glue that holds your team together, and they chart the direction in which your business will grow.

Begin by writing your five personal values.

1. _____

2. _____

3. _____

4. _____

5. _____

Then write five core business values.

1. _____

2. _____

3. _____

4. _____

5. _____

Note how they blend together to strengthen your business blueprint.

OUTLINING YOUR STANDARD OF ETHICS

Your ethics are as important as your values because your choice of ethics is an outline of how you and your advisory team will govern your business. These are your rules and standards of conduct, and they affect how decisions are made. Your ethics statements shape the way business will be done, and they should include what is good for both the individual and your community. Ethical behavior is based on the written and unwritten codes expected by society.

Below, create ten ethics statements that define how you intend to govern your business. Will you give people their money back and rip up their contracts if they can't afford to pay? Will you dig in your heels and make your clients press forward in misery? How will you handle the situation if you have two people on your advisory team who disagree about the direction you choose to take your business? What will you do when you pay for a service but the service worker doesn't perform? These are the questions built around ethics and how you intend to run your business.

1. _____

2. _____

3. _____

4. _____

5. _____

6. _____

7. _____

8. _____

9. _____

10. _____

BUILDING YOUR ADVISORY TEAM

A great advisory team is your best asset for the protection of your hard-earned money. This is the dream team that keeps you out of trouble legally and guides you throughout the years to become a viable company. It costs you nothing to consult with each of your potential advisory team players.

When running your own business, you may be tempted to wear many hats—janitor, accountant, salesperson, marketer, IT person, etc. Dr. John Demartini suggests that entrepreneurs not do anything they do not do well. Many solopreneurs decide to do it all and learn as they go along, but this holds you back from working on what you're good at. That is why you need an advisory team. Let the experts on your team do what they do best while you focus on doing what you love to do that makes you money.

When deciding who will be on your advisory team, I advise you not to hire your friends, someone who is cheap, or the first person you meet when choosing advisory team members. They must agree with your values, goals, and ethics statements while providing guidance for business growth.

Take the time to devise an arsenal of questions before meeting individually with your potential advisory team members. This will allow you to learn a lot about how to develop and deal with the challenges of forming your foundation. It will also provide an opportunity to fill in some unexpected steps in your business blueprint that you may not be aware of.

SUGGESTED ADVISORY TEAM MEMBERS

Accountant: Look for a great accountant, one who understands and is aware of what you can and cannot write off. It may take a number of interviews to find the right person because a good accountant is rare and worth his or her weight in gold. Find an accountant who understands what it means to be an entrepreneur. One of my most important questions is, "What are your thoughts on write-offs? Would you be willing to write off the room I have my office in? Usually, I write off a percentage of my mortgage (rental) expense because I work out of my home." If the person says no, then you are speaking with an accountant who is by the book and may not be comfortable with creative business write-offs.

If you take the time to complete this step, you'll save thousands of dollars and keep more money in your pocket. I make it a point to check in with my accountant before I make big financial decisions that may trigger a taxable event. Knowing he is there for this purpose provides safety for my business and peace of mind.

This is not a job for H&R Block, and don't even consider doing your taxes yourself. I cringe when I hear about entrepreneurs filing their own taxes. They are misguided into thinking they're saving money. Filing taxes themselves increases their liability and they have no one to fall back on for support if the IRS does come calling. Worst of all, they miss a lot of write-offs.

Bookkeeper: Your bookkeeper will keep track of your numbers and provide a profit-and-loss statement every month so you know where you stand financially. It's impossible to keep your business in the black if you have no idea how much money you are making and how much you incur in expenses. Ask around for references from friends and family who found a reputable bookkeeper. Be sure to get recent references from a bookkeeper you are considering hiring. What I appreciate about my bookkeeper is that she takes responsibility for following up, resolving her errors without charging me, and doesn't nickel and dime me for phone conversations.

Your bookkeeper should also work well with your accountant. Mine works so well with my accountant that she files my taxes and I don't do anything at tax time other than review my tax return and sign on the dotted line. My bookkeeper has been with me for more than twenty years and treats my business like it's her own.

Business Attorney: Even though you may not often need a business attorney, it's always good to have one on your team when you need one. For years, I had very little need for my business attorney, but when there was a liability issue, he was ready to defend me immediately. He stepped in and stopped the challenge from moving any further. There's nothing worse than getting sued and then looking for an attorney to answer questions and defend you when he doesn't know you. Think ahead and be prepared.

When interviewing business attorneys, you can do it on the phone, in person, or on Skype. The first consultation is usually free so it's a great time to get your legal questions answered. If you are considering a corporation or LLC, explain who you are and what you provide, as a business, for your clients. Ask your prospective lawyer about your liability and what he might consider for protection. If he tells you to create a C Corp and you have no employees, you've got the wrong attorney.

Virtual Assistants: Virtual assistants can be hired based on whatever your needs are at the time. I have a social-media assistant in the United States and a web developer in India. Ask around before hiring. Look for someone who speaks your language, someone you don't have to train, and someone who has the time to get the job done quickly.

For small things, use Fiverr.com. Read the reviews carefully for each provider in the genre you are selecting. Make sure the person speaks a language you understand, and ask how long it will take to get the work completed before you hire him or her.

Coaches:

Rule 1: Always hire a coach for accountability and guidance.

Rule 2: Never violate Rule 1.

I usually have two coaches at all times: one for the techie stuff and one for the business. You don't know what you don't know. A coach is paramount unless you are on a tightly defined course, and never, ever get distracted by bright, shiny objects and new programs that sound good in that moment. If this situation applies to you, then you get a high-five, but I've never seen anyone that lucky.

SELECTING YOUR BUSINESS SUCCESS COACH

Whom you hire as a business success coach will either make or break your business. It doesn't matter who you are or how big you get; you will always need a qualified business coach to take you to the next level.

Below are my twelve well-defined steps to assist in the selection of your next business coach or trainer. I suggest you review this list each time you're in the position of making this decision.

1. Do your due diligence and check credentials. Just because a coach says she can show you how to make seven figures doesn't mean she ever has, ever will, or can now.

2. Make sure the coach you hire is also a great mentor. She should have already done the painful tacking back and forth while making those golden mistakes, so she can warn and direct you in saving valuable time and money.

3. Find out how many years a coach has been in business before hiring her.

4. Look for and watch videos and written testimonials provided by her clients.

5. Don't let anyone tell you credentials aren't required. Credentials build trust in the public eye. If the coach has had years of training and experience but no credentials, you may be all right. Ask around.

6. If the coach's experience is minimal, ask about her credentials. Talk with her clients. A lot of great programs are out there, but hiring an intuitive coach who is able to work specifically in your area of expertise to build your business is golden.

7. Don't put the cart before the horse. Forget the branding and marketing before finding out whether what you want to sell will be acceptable to your target market or any target market. Ask what steps the coach suggests to assist you in building your business. If she says branding and marketing should be completed before defining your target market and researching the needs of your clients, run in the other direction. I frequently meet with business owners who have all of their branding and websites ready to go but no programs to sell. This means all of their money has been flowing out of their

bank accounts and little, if any, has been gushing in.

8. Avoid spending thousands with a coach who is beta-testing a program. Beta programs should be inexpensive because the program is newly developed and the coach isn't yet clear on the results or how to teach it. If you are made aware of and choose to participate in a beta program, you must be okay with the risk of spending money on an unknown outcome and giving up the time without a clear benefit. On the other hand, you can get some awesome training at an inexpensive price, so it's important to think carefully and weigh your options.

    Be thoughtful about your next step in business and hire a coach who provides specific answers to your immediate needs. Here's an example: I made the decision it was time to complete my book, get it edited, and put it into production. My intention was to stop speaking for free and begin moving into the next level of becoming a powerful keynote speaker. I searched a year for the right coach, looking carefully to see whether each one was actively performing the vision of where I wanted to go. Finally, one evening I happened upon Patrick Snow and hired him immediately. Many coaches could have shown me how to publish my book, but they had no idea how to move into becoming a valued keynote speaker. Patrick provided the answer and is an active keynote speaker, which met with my intentions of what I wanted to do.

9. Don't let anyone point out your weaknesses or intimidate you into believing you need his or her services. This is a big red flag.

10. Ask about the coach's experience and philosophies around defining your title, creating programs, and an easy-sell, structured-pricing procedure. This is the key to making you money. Without this expertise, you have almost no way of

making money. Once your programs are developed, will this person be able to guide you in a way that you'll know what to say to make your business enticing to your target market?

CERTIFICATES, DEGREES, AND THE BEE'S KNEES

A big part of your foundation is built on your certifications, degrees, and your backstory. The general public thrives on certifications and degrees, and seeing them alongside your name builds trust almost immediately, provided they understand what the abbreviations mean. I've seen some real estate cards with so many abbreviations that they only cause confusion because the general public has no understanding of their meanings.

My CFE Certified Financial Educator® certification has opened a great many doors for me because there are only 253 of us in the United States licensed to teach on business and university campuses. What doors will your credentials open for you?

At one time, I worked with coaches who work as a couple. They suggested I drop my designation and informed me that credentials and certifications aren't important. Perhaps they said this because they didn't have any designations. They have built their business and sell their programs based on their backstory, which is also acceptable if you have years of experience and can prove what you know works.

List your certifications, degrees, and/or backstory. _____

_____

_____

_____

_____

INCORPORATING QUESTIONS

At some point, you will need to set up a corporation as a liability and tax strategy. When I started my multi-million-dollar nation-wide company, I ran it as a sole proprietorship the first year and ended up paying the IRS $100,000. It was so painful to write that check that I had to drive through East San Jose's dilapidated neighborhoods to appreciate what I had. As I wrote the check, my hand was shaking and I vowed I would never get caught in a squeeze like that again. I formed a California C Corporation the very next month.

A number of options exist for deciding on which corporation to form, each one's purpose, and the costs. If you want to research the best entity for your personal business strategy, I suggest you read *Own Your Own Corporation* by Garrett Sutton. He does an excellent job of laying out your options in a way that's easy to understand. Then you can go to your business attorney and have him set up the corporation that suits your business best, after consulting with your accountant.

Throughout this chapter, we've been working together to build your business foundation and your millionaire blueprint. Please don't underestimate the importance of these steps. They are essentially the backbone of your business, and without them, you may be completely unaware and caught off-guard if an unexpected situation arises. Our goal is to make sure your business takes the important steps that catapult you out of the hobby zone and into a sustaining income-generating machine.

"You will get all you want in life if you help enough other people get what they want."

— Zig Ziglar

♡

CHAPTER 4

Succeeding with Client Communication

Completing the steps in your foundation can go on for months, so don't feel bad if your blueprint is not completed immediately. Actually, completing it immediately is not possible, and not having it finished shouldn't hold you back from developing your programs and learning how to market and relate to potential clients.

If you want to expand and grow your business, you have two options. You can grow by conquering, pushing, and consistently reviewing your profit sheets. But there's another way—an easier way, a kinder and more-caring way. You can grow by building lifelong relationships with people who become friends, who believe in your service, and who love working with you. In this way, you work and flow with the Universe and everyone wins.

While living on Maui, I had an opportunity to sit on the beach and chat with Michael Singer, author of *The Untethered Soul*. As we sat drenched in the energy of the waves lapping up on shore, he made a profound statement I've never forgotten. We were chatting about my unexpected impending divorce, the sadness and disappointment I had internalized, and the next best steps for my future when he said, "People are watching to see what you do." Until he made this statement, it hadn't occurred to me that each one of us is a role model for others to follow, and what you do and say during the most difficult trials in life reflects on your integrity and how others see you.

Unfortunately, it's mostly the bad behaviors people talk about. If you believe you are right about something and decide you must make it known and hurt someone's feelings, that person will back away and take everyone he knows with him. It's your choice to look deep within for a vision of what's to come before acting and reaping the pain when others check out of your life.

All of the formulas in this book were developed as a standard to support you in developing a personality that will attract clients who want to work with you. You will learn that the way you act toward others will, in turn, be how others will react to you. Perhaps there are times when it just isn't worth being right, so let it go.

DEVELOPING AN AUTHENTIC CHARACTER YOUR CLIENTS WILL LOVE

In his book *The Law of Success in 16 Lessons*[1], Napoleon Hill explains why it's important to develop an authentic character:

> Remember that your *reputation* is made by others, but your *character* is made by *you*!
>
> You want your reputation to be a favorable one, but you cannot be sure that it will be for the reason that it is something that exists outside of your own control, in the minds of others. It is what others believe you to be. With your character

---

1 "Lesson 16: The Golden Rule." Meriden, CT: Ralston UP, 1928. p. 39.

it is different. Your character is that which *you are*, as the results of your *thoughts* and *deeds*. You control it. You can make it weak, good or bad. When you are satisfied and know in your mind that your character is above reproach you need not worry about your reputation, for it is as impossible for your character to be destroyed or damaged by anyone except yourself as it is to destroy matter or energy.

Have you ever wondered or even thought about who you are in the sales process and how others see and experience you? Are people excited when you walk in the door, or do they try to avoid eye contact and stay away?

My clients feel a myriad of emotions that you might identify with. Many of them are scared to death to interact because they don't know how to begin a sales conversation without feeling sales-y and pushy. I just experienced someone pushy like this two days ago at a seminar. When I walked in the door, a woman practically tackled me. Well, not really, but it felt that way. We'd never met before, and she didn't even take the time to introduce herself before shoving a flyer in my hand and insisting that I had to write a book. She then proceeded to tell me her six reasons why I should start writing today. Sadly, I'll probably make every effort not to get corralled by her again so there will be no opportunity to share the news that my book was just about to be published. Have you ever experienced a salesperson like this? Are you one yourself?

Other clients are afraid of sales because they have been rejected a few times. We'll talk more about this later, but I want you to know that it's okay to be rejected because it makes you stronger. Asking for the money, answering questions in lieu of overcoming objections, and making money are all part of the sales process. But I have a secret for you: If you begin by understanding who your clients are and you learn how to work with their specific personality types, it will make all the difference in how your clients interact with and perceive you.

Let's look at these personality types now so you can begin making adjustments in how you envision yourself, during the process, in relation to your clients.

DEFINING CLIENTS BY PERSONALITY TYPES

In an attempt to make the definitions of the personalities easier to understand, I'm introducing you to them in layers. In this chapter, I'll introduce you to layer one, and in the chapters that follow, to layers two and three.

Layer one is the easiest to identify. The personalities in it are grouped as being either Big Picture/Visionary or Step-by-Step People. In this layer, you'll learn how to identify these personalities easily, how to interact with them, and why each one is important to the other.

Once you've determined how your client relates to the first layer, we'll define the second layer, which identifies the personalities according to the DISC for Sales profile. With this layer, you'll discover the secrets for how to identify each of the four personality types by their surroundings, their pace of speech, and the words they use. You'll learn how to interact with each personality type and gain insights into their needs.

The third layer teaches you how to call your clients to you, rather than you chasing them. This layer shows you how to recognize each personality according to the types of words and phrases those clients use and which words and phrases they are waiting to hear from you. This technique is one many sales courses miss completely, and it gives you a big advantage. With this information, you can walk into a networking group of only twelve people and walk away with three new clients after only a one-minute introduction. This layer provides the lean-in "He or she gets me" know-how that we can use from the stage, in marketing, or during interviews.

This technique includes:

- The "why" people—those who want to know why they should want your product or service.

- The "how" people—those who want to know how your product or service works.

- The "what" people—those who want to know what your product or service is, including a description of all its bells and whistles.

Let's begin with layer one. If you take your time to learn each layer thoroughly, you'll be way ahead of your competition and it will make a world of difference in your income.

Layer 1: Big Picture People vs. Step-By-Step People

Two types of clients show up in your database and circulate around you on earth: big-picture visionaries and step-by-steps. Each has a distinct perspective and deep-seated core beliefs. As you walk through life, I guarantee every person you interact with falls into one of these two groups. Each is divinely rooted in skills the other often doesn't possess, and one is frequently not capable of completing a mission without the other. Which group a client comfortably fits into makes a big difference during the sales process, as does how you choose to communicate with him and meet his needs.

There have been all kinds of theories about personality types, but in my opinion, narrowing it down to these two types is easier to decipher and remember. Later, we'll go into a deeper study of the four personality types during the sales process, but first let's examine these two types:

Big-Picture Visionaries

Big-picture people may also be identified as visionaries. These people have a vision of whatever they are attempting to accomplish. They are able to see clearly, in their own minds, all of the moving pieces and how they fit together. Where they come up short is in implementing the step-by-step process for how to get there. Here is where the step-by-step people excel and carry the project through to the end.

Big-picture people are generally bottom-line people, and once they design the end result, they are done and move on to the next project, leaving the details to a step-by-step team.

While big-picture people are working on developing the vision, they might become agitated and annoyed with interruptions and idle chit-chat because they hold such big visions in their heads. These people frequently hold positions such as CEOs, leaders, inventors, and business owners.

Step-By-Steps

Step-by-step people are very important to big-picture people because they are detail-oriented and will take on the task of figuring out how to reach the goal. They will not skip a step, and they take a great deal of time, effort, and pride in determining the best and most efficient route to the requested result. Their diligence and pace will frequently cause a big-picture person to feel the project is moving too slowly.

Step-by-step people love to share and chitchat about what they're working on. They're great about asking for support on how to complete a task if they feel stumped. They may express annoyance if a big-picture person paints the vision and pushes them into a project without providing finely outlined steps to reach the desired result. In fact, step-by-steps become quickly overwhelmed if they're given too much information at once, and they may even completely shut down.

Step-by-steps would much rather have an outline, an Excel spreadsheet, or a 1-2-3 set of steps to reach their goals. They would prefer to be given only one step at a time, if possible, and their instructions must be clearly defined. Examples of people who fit into this personality type would be planners, engineers, accountants, paralegals, secretaries, and escrow officers.

Big-picture people practice what I call "chunking it up." This means they take a massive project, break it into manageable chunks, and delegate those chunks to team managers. The managers each take their pieces, instruct their step-by-step teams on how to accomplish the goals, and then report back to the big-picture person on the project's progress.

Communication between big-picture people and step-by-step people is frequently strained because the big-picture person can't understand why a step-by-step person can't relate to his vision, and the step-by-step person is confused and afraid she won't understand the vision, and won't do the job correctly if she doesn't have the steps to reach the big-picture result.

Clarifying Communication Between the Two Basic Personality Types

Step-by-steps need all of the intricate details before understanding how to get to the end result. Here's the rub: Visionaries often don't know all of the details, and what worsens the situation is that the details aren't important to them. They simply see the vision and leave it to others to figure out how to get there.

This need for communication between the two types is precisely why managers are important. Managers are the go-betweens and communicators who keep both types of people happy. It's important to know yourself and how you play in the world of business. Which personality type are you?

I'm a big-picture person, so I find it very difficult to sit for hours writing and automating classes. It's really not my thing. However, at times, I'm required to do this type of work because no one else can write my classes for me. I can fit into either personality type, but I am more comfortable leading a team as a big-picture person.

It's rare that a person is a blend of both traits and can easily utilize the skills of both. It is, however, a lot easier to set up business systems and processes, while holding the vision yourself because there's clarity around how it all comes together and you can see the ultimate destination and where you're going all at the same time.

Applying Clarification to Sales

A big-picture person wants the bottom line first, and then you can move to telling him how your product or service will benefit him. He has no interest in the systems you set up to get to the benefits, and he will quickly tire and make an excuse to flee the conversation if you launch into the details. This is why it's so important for you to know exactly how to get to the bottom line by describing your business in thirty succinct seconds. Usually after the third sentence, you've already lost him.

Bottom line means minimal words that make a big impact. Here's an example of what I use for my business: "I teach entrepreneurs how to create massive visibility for massive income." Short and sweet! My Business Mastery Platinum course includes a mastermind that supports you in creating a succint thirty-second description of your business. It's important to define your business in a way that gets people's attention and says exactly what you do all at the same time. Once this promo has been created, it can be used at all of your networking events and interviews as a succinct description of what you do. You can view Celebrity Guest Expert red carpet promos on my website if you'd like to see videos displaying what graduates have used as their thirty-second promos.

See whether you can get your business description down to five to seven words. The root of what I say is, "Creating Massive Visibility for Massive Income." Six words say it all. With step-by-step people, it's better to be prepared with the nitty-gritty, all the details, each benefit, and the reasons why it will benefit or be a good fit for them. They might even want statistics to back up your statements, and they may feel cheated and not willing to move forward if you don't give them enough information. They frequently ask for reading material and will run to the Internet to check out your product, just to make sure. Don't get insulted. That's just how they are.

Observing Personality Behaviors

Write down the names of three important people in your life or three clients you want to do business with. See whether you can identify each one as a big-picture person or a step-by-step person. Next to each name, indicate whether he or she is a big-picture person, a step-by-step person, or both. Think very carefully about each person and how you've been relating to him or her. Next, write what you might do differently to enhance each relationship or change the way you will do business with each person in the future based on their personality type.

Person 1:

_____

_____

_____

_____

Person 2:

_____

_____

_____

_____

Person 3:

_____

_____

_____

_____

This exercise will make a big difference in your sales effectiveness if you are able to utilize it to build relationships and recognize whom you are speaking with. Understanding and developing this practice will make money rain on you because you'll easily become aware of how to develop and work with your team and your clients to make more sales.

"What you get by achieving your goals is not as important as what you become by achieving your goals."

— Zig Ziglar

♡

CHAPTER 5

The Secret to Selling Authentically

During my twenty-eight-year education in sales, I have practiced more than 1,000 times to get the sales process right. I've tried other people's scripts, and I've been yelled at and pressured by superiors, disappointed by clients, discouraged, taken advantage of, and cheated out of sales commissions.

While building my multi-million-dollar business, I learned no one likes to feel pushed and prodded to produce sales. The most painful thing to witness is great people breaking down in tears and feeling defeated when they could be loved, supported, and rewarded into producing great results.

It's not the fault of the salespeople. It's the disastrous misuse of the training provided. Sure, the training works for some, but the majority of people don't resonate with hard-sell, pushy tactics. Then, after months of training, time, and expense, salespeople quit and run away, feeling defeated, angry, and in pain.

You might say, "I hate sales. Even my family and friends won't buy from me. I just can't take the rejection, and I don't like feeling pushy. Besides, I don't even know how to start a sales conversation."

But what if you had a mentor who had already made most of the mistakes, spent the money, and could save you years of time? What if you could learn tips like "If you don't want to feel rejected, never attempt to sell to family and friends"?

That would be a good thing to know, wouldn't it? That is exactly why I wrote this book. Twenty-eight years of being in sales has presented me with 1,000 lessons, so if you can stay focused and read to the end, you'll save a great deal of time and money getting your business out of the hobby zone.

Sales is not about scripts, pushing others into buying something they don't want or need, using sales-y phrases, feeling the pain of rejection, or running from one networking group to the next without results. Sales is about being authentic, building relationships, speaking a language your clients can understand, following a tested system that gets results, and focusing on the benefits your clients are looking for.

Did you know your people are waiting for you? The problem is they don't know where to find you because you haven't learned how to step up where they can see you. I bet you've been so focused on looking for your clients that you haven't even noticed they're right in front of you.

The main problem is that most solopreneurs don't take the time to research and define their target market and define their needs before creating and attempting to sell their programs. They set themselves up for failure.

Other problems include the fear of sales, knowing who they are in the sales process, and knowing how to relate to the different personality types they'll be interacting with. Pulling all of this information together to develop the skills necessary to build an income-generating business is imperative to solopreneur success. The next layer will assist you in identifying the needs of your perfect clients and how you can easily relate to them.

Layer 2: Identifying Your Clients Through DISC

After researching the various personality-typing products on the market, it became clear to me that if I could manipulate the DISC program to suit the sales process, it would be (and is) the perfect solution for evaluating and understanding how to work with your clients authentically.

DISC is considered to be a "universal language of behavior" that, once learned, allows you to "read" and relate to the different personality types. Being "DISC-literate" means you know how each personality style differs from the rest. This insight transforms every client-sales relationship into an authentic, heartfelt, genuine connection.

DISC Sales is based on a four-quadrant model representing the four recurring behavioral patterns that are typically used. Dr. William Marston's landmark scientific research was done in the 1920s in America. At that time, he classified the four recurring patterns of observable behavior in normal (vs. abnormal or insane) human behavior and named them with the scientifically accurate, observable behavioral terms: "Dominance, Influence, Steadiness, and Compliance."

Organizations large and small have been using similar self-administered, twelve-minute input surveys to assist them in hiring the right support personnel, so I suggest we follow their lead. Once you have had an opportunity to review your DISC Sales report, you will immediately understand your own behaviors better and how you relate to others.

In my course Compel Don't Sell: The Art of Selling With Heart, you receive five video-instruction modules that teach the meaning of your personal sales profile and how you can relate perfectly to each of the other three personality types. If you'd like to take the DISC Sales profile and learn about who you are in the sales process, go to ShirleneReeves.com to take the On-Demand DISC Sales Profile Assessment.

As you review your profile, you'll see you may have two or three of the personality types in your graph that are high. We all have more than one personality type within us, but there is always a dominant one.

Discovering You in the Sales Process

The purpose of this important step is to provide the ability to speak to audiences in a way that calls your clients to you, and the best way to begin understanding your clients is to begin understanding yourself.

It should only take about twelve minutes to answer the profile questions and, within fifteen minutes, your DISC Sales profile will be delivered to your email inbox.

Although you may have taken other profiling programs, the DISC Sales Profile has been designed specifically for sales and how you relate to others in the sales process. It's entirely different from any other profiler. Don't be fooled into thinking you've already taken one. I promise you haven't, unless you've attended one of my courses. No one else offers this specifically designed profile.

As you move through the questions, don't dwell on them or try to figure out what the answers *should* be. Choose the answer that pops into your mind first. It shouldn't take any longer than twelve minutes to complete the profile questions.

I have found that when my students take the DISC Sales Profile during their pre-training course, they are more open and available for coaching because of the personal insights they see printed within their personal reports.

Once all the students in a group have taken their profiles and shared their distinctions, they feel understood and valued just for being who they are in a way most have never before experienced.

This process provides clarity for why you were called to choose the business you do and why you feel so comfortable and excited about your passion. Armed with the power of knowledge, your profile proves it's easier to take the steps necessary to apply your natural strengths and to request coaching on the weaknesses that might be holding you back.

Suddenly, you will begin to see and give a name, priority, and focus to your own recurring patterns of behavior. You'll see why you've developed certain strengths and why they have developed over the years through unquestioned use.

You will begin to see what led to your behavioral style and the patterns you tend to be most comfortable using. While reviewing the graphs, you'll get clarity on how to adapt or change a given behavior if it isn't useful in accomplishing your goals or building client relationships.

Many of my students become DISC certified because the profiles are so effective as a tool for understanding their clients. A great many coaches gain quick insights into effective coaching simply by requiring that their clients pay a small fee to take their profile questionnaire online. The report is received by both the client and his or her coach, and within minutes, the client receives beneficial coaching insights that make a difference in coaching efficiency and quickly benefit the client with life shifts and ahas—something that without the personality profile assesment might have taken years to determine.

This is why I find these profiles so effective. Everyone is different and, as a business-success expert, it's imperative that I coach my clients in a way that allows us to relate to and understand each other easily and effectively. The DISC Sales Profile Assessment provides for this ease of communication between my students and me. There are other on-demand profiles you can use for other client specific needs as a coach at ShirleneReeves.com.

"You have to get along with people, but you also have to recognize that the strength of a team is different people with different perspectives and different personalities."

— Steve Case

♡

CHAPTER 6

Discovering Whom You Are Dealing With

Because the DISC Sales Profiling System can give people a deeper understanding of the many dimensions of behavior, my students use it to gain insights into and connect better with their clients. This process shortens the "trial and error" phase of getting to know someone, reduces assumptions, and provides clarity while creating more confidence during the sales process.

Through the DISC sales techniques, you'll discover people speak a common language and each of the four DISC personalities, which we will look at more closely in a moment, coincides with easy, identifiable, basic behaviors. This is why professional coaches, trainers, speakers, and leaders of highly conscious organizations appreciate becoming DISC-literate and want to share their knowledge with their teams. With this program, you can start new relationships by getting clear on the DISC styles and preferences, first within you and then by learning how to identify and work with your clients.

Applying DISC Distinctions to Sales

The DISC Behavioral Style Model is based on the needs that motivate a person and the person's patterns of behavior that are observable by watching his or her interactions. The more comfortable a person is in a situation, the easier it is to identify that person's natural style.

When you meet someone for the first time, she may anticipate that you are going to try to sell her something, so she will become guarded, which might make it more difficult to identify her primary DISC behavior. However, a person's primary style isn't hard to learn if you know what to look for.

Look at the list of behavioral styles below and see whether you can identify the styles of the people who currently surround you. Once you become familiar with the traits of each personality type, you'll easily be able to recognize them in your clients. Hint: If a person's behavior doesn't measure up to any of the following identifying factors and shows up as the complete opposite, it's probably because of the intensity of the person's need rather than emotion or fear.

Identifying Four DISC Behavioral Styles

1. Dominance: High "D" Style

   - Decisive actions and decisions
   - Likes control, dislikes inaction
   - Prefers maximum freedom to manage himself and others
   - Cool, independent, and competitive
   - Low tolerance for feelings, attitudes, and advice of others
   - Works quickly and impressively alone
   - Good administrative skills

2. Interactive, Influencer: High "I" Style

    - Spontaneous actions and decisions
    - Likes involvement
    - Dislikes being alone
    - Exaggerates and generalizes
    - Tends to dream and gets others caught up in his/her dreams
    - Jumps from one activity to another
    - Works quickly and excitedly with others
    - Seeks esteem and acknowledgment
    - Good persuasive skills

3. Steadiness: High "S" Style

    - Slow at taking action and making decisions
    - Likes close, personal relationships
    - Dislikes interpersonal conflict
    - Supports and actively listens to others
    - Weak at goal setting and self-direction
    - Has excellent ability to gain support from others
    - Works slowly and cohesively with others
    - Seeks security and belongingness
    - Good interaction skills

4. Conscientious: High "C" Style

    - Cautious actions and decisions
    - Likes organization and structure
    - Dislikes involvement
    - Asks many questions about specific details
    - Prefers objective, task-oriented, intellectual work environment
    - Wants to be right, so can be overly reliant on data collection
    - Works slowly and precisely alone
    - Good problem-solving skills

You may already be thinking about whom you know who fits into each personality type. Let's look at each of these styles individually.

High D Personalities are:

Dominant—Driving—Demanding—Doing

High D personalities, also known as Dominants, display a strong, commanding management style and are frequently known to be bossy and controlling. Often, it's their way or the highway. They attempt to shape their environments to overcome obstacles on their paths to reaching desired goals and accomplishments. They demand the freedom to manage themselves and those who surround them, and they are great at using their well-designed delegation skills to accomplish their goals.

These assertive types tend to appear cool, independent, and competitive. They opt for measurable results, including their own personal worth, as determined by their personal track records. They are the best at initiating change and are much like the lion, the leader of the animal kingdom: number one.

High Ds in the Workplace

When entering a Dominant Style's office, look around. The overall tone suggests authority and control. Their desks may be covered with projects and papers, stacked in neat piles.

They tend to surround themselves with trophies, awards, and other evidence of personal achievement. Virtually everything about the place suggests hustle, bustle, formality, and power. You may see a large chair behind a massive desk. Besides non-verbally announcing "I'm important," the desk keeps visitors at a distance and is a symbol of intimidation.

Dominant Styles enjoy the constant activity of hustle, bustle, and competition, so you'll seldom catch them idle. Between existing tasks, they pick up new ones. They perk up when competing and appear to thrive with pressure-cooker schedules. They often squeeze you onto their calendars and let you know their time is limited, either by telling you outright or by looking at or fiddling with their watches. If they're finished with your conversation, they frequently shift their gazes elsewhere, or make and take phone calls while you sit in their office.

These people often walk with a quick pace in pursuit of a tangible goal and may not even acknowledge you in passing. They are brisk and brusque without realizing it.

When under stress, impatience emerges and they may push others aside to reach their goals. When pressure intensifies, Dominant Styles often rise to the occasion. Under time constraints, they may concede to impatience and rely on educated guesses or a hunch that isn't to be second-guessed.

Dominant Styles let people know they've made it without having to say so. They keep possessions in plain sight that emit the message of their success and authority, such as owning a black or steel-gray Mercedes or BMW. Maybe a Sherman tank would be better suited to this personality style.

Voicemail Message Tips for High Ds are:

- Give your phone number at beginning and end
- Articulate clearly at a quick rate of speech
- Tell them exactly what you are calling about
- Tell them exactly what you want them to do
- Let them know what to expect in the next step

If you are emailing a High D, use this email sales example:

Debbie,

I know you're constantly looking for ways to increase business and leverage sales to gain a competitive edge over your competition. Click here to read a hard-hitting article that teaches how to leverage your business to create more sales and high-touch client relationships.

Success always,

When speaking on the phone to a Dominant Style, treat him or her the same way you would during a person-to-person contact. Think of the ABCs: Keep it abridged, brief, and concise. Then prepare for your delivery with the bottom line in mind. For example:

"The trend in your industry is toward computer-generated graphics. The research we've conducted with other typesetters in your area indicates increased profits of 20 to 30 percent over two years. I'd like to meet with you for ten minutes to show you the numbers and see whether this concept interests you."

It's not uncommon for Dominant Styles to launch into a phone conversation without even a hello. They tend to get right to the point. "What were you thinking? How could you charge that person for a program without talking to me first?" The Dominant may perceive the person on the other end of the line as incompetent if he isn't able to keep up with the speed of information and questioning.

You'll know whether you have a Dominant Style on the phone simply by listening for power signals. He will choose the time and place to meet and often speak in concise, pointed statements with a cool, confident, and demanding tone.

A Dominant Style may call and say, "Andrea? Debbie? Alicia there?" Talking to this person is like speaking to a human text. She reduces the concept of "brief and to the point" to another dimension. As commanding speakers who tend not to listen to others, Dominants direct all conversations toward their personal agendas and goals.

Under stress, a Dominant can become defensive and aggressive, attacking others to demonstrate who's in control. These people are not touchy-feely and prefer sensible-thinking terminology. You might hear, "I think this conversation is over. I'm done. You can go now." If you find yourself in a tangle with one, you probably won't win, and even if you think you won the battle, the Dominant will never agree.

High I Personalities are:

Influential—Impressive—Interactive—Inspiring—Initiating

High Is exhibit enthusiasm, persuasiveness, friendliness, and are often big picture visionaries who may have the ability to blend in step-by-step skills. They provide great ideas and are successful at getting others to come on board to support their dreams and missions. They have a natural preference for talking and listening in terms of feelings. Unconsciously, they may become uncomfortable and confused when talking to a person who uses thinking words. (The opposite is also true). Statements like, "I feel like we should have had a say about the change in plans," or "I feel good about what we've accomplished today," tend to put these people-oriented types more at ease.

With great persuasion, Interactives influence others and shape their environments by building alliances and communities to accomplish results for the benefit of all involved.

Interactives ask for comments and feedback of approval to make sure the team is comfortable moving in the same direction. These people are stimulating, talkative, and communicative. They can be much like a porpoise—playful, sociable, talkative, and impressive.

High Is in the Workplace

When entering the workplace of a High I, you may see paperwork strewn across her desk and all over the floor. It looks like a cluttered, disorganized mess, and if you comment, "How do you find anything?" the Interactive will probably respond by saying it's a system of disorganized organization because she knows exactly where everything is.

If you decide to support a High I by organizing his paperwork into piles, he'll flip out because he'll no longer be able to find anything. Interactives want everything laid out where they can see and access it easily.

You may find prestigious awards such as liberal arts degrees, motivational or upbeat slogans, generalized personal comments, or stimulating posters on the walls, along with Post-It notes taped everywhere within view with little apparent forethought, rhyme, or reason. Their overall decor reflects an open, airy, lively atmosphere that reveals an answer to who they are as individuals.

The furniture tends to be informal, inviting, and warm. Interactives rarely sit behind desks while engaging with others, and they frequently opt for comfortable, accessible seating. In fact, they might take a seat next to you at a table or on a couch in an effort to see and hear you better while getting a feel for how you respond. These people are talkative, emotional and animated.

Style of Dress

The way Interactive Styles dress often relates to their need for recognition. Since they like others to notice them, they may dress in the latest styles with glitz and pizzazz—look at me! Interactive Styles like bright colors and unusual clothes that prompt others to compliment or comment on them. Many Interactives even prefer negative comments to none at all. "Are you dressed for Halloween today, Jennifer?"

The color red seems to rank number one with Interactive Styles as their color of choice for clothes, cars, or convertibles. They like glamour, flash, and excitement.

Voicemail Message Tips for High Is are:

- Use a warm, expressive tone of voice
- Be upbeat with high energy
- Suggest a meeting where you can share ideas
- Give them your "private" number
- Let them know the first meeting is an opportunity to get to know each other

If you are emailing a High I, use this email sales example:

Dear Michael,

I know you're big into sending out info that increases top-of-mind awareness with your clients, prospects, and affiliates. That's what makes you so successful!

Check out this cool article that teaches how to leverage high-tech to stay in meaningful contact with hundreds of people in your database.

Let me know what you think!

Best,

Conversational Tips

Influencers begin their conversations with "Hey, what's up?" or "How are things?" They use a lot of vocal inflections/intonations, and the words they use may feel somewhat exaggerated. "Really? That's awesome!" or "No way. Are you kidding?"

While talking with them on the phone or visiting their homes, you may hear background noises and sounds coming from the TV or radio. Interactives enjoy visual stimulation. They speak rapidly in feeling terms. "I feel like writing a chapter in an anthology will be a waste of time and money and won't accomplish my goals. I have a strong feeling that I need to write my own book." They use the word *feel* instead of *think*, which tends to be a favorite of the other three personality types.

Typically, you'll notice a wide range of vocal inflection and intonation with them, and it's important that you react to it because that's what they expect. "Do you feel that way, too?" They liven up conversations with personal anecdotes and stories, and they may keep you on the phone longer than you anticipated.

If you need to get on with your day and need to get off the phone, try something like, "Well, Julia, it's been great talking with you. I'm really looking forward to our appointment on Tuesday!" Say it with feeling and the Interactive Style will look forward to your meeting and let you go.

High S Personalities are:

Supportive—Steady—Sensible—Stable—Serving

As a rule, a High S, also known as a Steady, will have a soothing voice with a calm, comfortable delivery. Steady Styles are easy to get along with, laid back, and usually go with the flow. They prefer stable relationships, which don't jeopardize anyone or rock the boat, especially when it comes to themselves.

The koala bear that hangs out on a tree limb for hours represents the steady style of a High S. Steady Styles are slower to make decisions, agonizing for days over one choice, and even after they make that choice, they'll often go back and evaluate it. However, once they make a decision, they will follow through at a slow and steady pace. Their disposition and appearance is approachable, warm, and friendly.

High Ss in the Workplace

When you enter a Steady Style's office, you'll find conservatively framed personal slogans, group photos, and serene landscapes. You'll also find family photos and special mementos, turned so they can view them from their desk chairs. They favor items that represent stabilizing memories, experiences, and relationships. These objects are reminders of a pleasant, uncomplicated past that transforms their work area into a friendly, warm ambience.

They prefer a side-by-side seating arrangement that allows for more cooperation. If there is a desk, they will come out from behind it to shake your hand for a more personal engagement.

You may see certificates on the walls recognizing volunteer hours for various hands-on activities in their community. Steady Styles typically enjoy giving their time to causes they feel strongly about. Aside from the possibility of meeting new potential friends, this activity also helps satisfy their need to see for themselves: (1) what's really going on, (2) where they fit into the group effort, and (3) how they can get meaningful, concrete results in their businesses.

This style is a natural born listener with slower patterns and a low-key delivery. Their questions often focus on concrete topics and experiences. "What did you say the terms for payment were again?" They walk casually, acknowledging others, and sometimes get sidetracked by old friends they might run across in public places.

Steady Styles dislike calling attention to themselves. They wear subdued colors and conservatively cut clothing, favoring conventional styles that don't stand out too much. They like beige or light blue economical cars like Passats or family-sized SUVs with factory-recommended tires. If they could get away with it, they wouldn't elect to pay for a horn. To Steady Styles, using a horn is like yelling at somebody; consequently, they also avoid loud music and opt for and enjoy songs with a steady, predictable, soothing flow like jazz, spa music, or show tunes.

Voicemail Message Tips for High Ss are:

- Breathe deeply and relax
- Smile as you speak warmly at a measured rate
- Be personable, yet professional
- Tell them who referred you
- Thank them in advance for returning your call

If you are emailing a High S, use this email sales example:

> Dear Annie,
>
> I know you care deeply about keeping your clients, helping others, and staying in contact with all of your prospects.
>
> I just found this article that teaches you how to increase your sales by using this high-tech program to create high-touch client relationships, and I wanted you to have the information, too.
>
> Feel free to call me if you want to discuss this personally.
>
> Warmly,

"How are you?" or "I'm glad to hear from you again," are typical Steady Style greetings. Although Steady Styles are warm and prefer more personal interactions, they'll also be okay with indirect contact—especially if the person is pleasant and non-threatening. They appreciate first-name relationships with callers even if they don't know them. "You don't have to be formal. Just call me Brenda." They communicate in a steady pace, and even their vocal intonations convey friendliness, comfort, and a sense of calm.

Steady Styles are naturals at listening to others' ideas and feelings, whether on the phone or in person. They tend to be interested in the blow-by-blow, point-by-point description of what you did yesterday or the step-by-step pattern of how to complete a certain task.

You're probably talking to a Steady Style if you notice slower than average speech patterns, more moments of listening than of speaking, and references to actual, real-life stories regarding their products or programs.

Members of this personality type tend to express themselves in a rather tentative manner in both face-to-face and telephone conversations. "Give me a minute to check my calendar before making a decision," or "I'm not sure I can do that, but I'll get back to you as soon as I find out."

These people frequently defer to operating step-by-step in a more human, proven way and will fall back on doing a task the way it's always been done rather than making a change. They typically feel more comfortable making decisions based on conferring with others rather than on their own. "What do you think?" and "What do you recommend?" are common questions the Steady type might ask.

High C Personalities are:

Conscientious—Competent—Creative—Curious—Coordinating

High C personalities, also known as Conscientious or Competent Styles, are all about accuracy, details, independence, clarification, dependability, and organization. They focus on policies, practices, procedures, expectations, and outcomes. They want to know how things work so they can correctly evaluate their functionality.

As a child, my oldest son spent the majority of his time dissecting his toys to see how they worked and spent very little time actually playing with them. Once they were disassembled, he'd walk away and leave the parts in a pile. If you see this in your child, he is definitely a High C. High Cs always want to know and define how a product or service works prior to purchasing it, and the best way to satisfy this desire is to be prepared with statistics and details when you connect with them during Step 2 of the Sales Waltz as outlined in Chapter 16.

High C personalities are stars when it comes to editing books, analyzing numbers, and working through step-by-step functioning to reach an intended goal. A fox would be the most appropriate animal for this clearly competent style because High Cs are curious, resourceful, and cautious. They have an instinctive need to be right, and they prefer checking things out themselves before making a decision or purchase.

High Cs in the Workplace

Competent, Conscientious Styles often carry their organizational tendencies into their work environments. Their desks are neat and highly organized with displays charts, graphs, exhibits, models, credentials, and work-related pictures placed neatly on their workplace walls or shelves. Everything has a special place, and if a stapler needs to be used, it will be returned immediately to its proper place. Competent Styles favor a functional decor that enables them to work more efficiently, and they tend to keep most objects within reach to be readily available when needed. Where appropriate, you may notice state-of-the-art technology to enhance their efficiency.

It isn't always easy to communicate with this personality style. They speak in short sentences with pertinently chosen words and would prefer to ask questions rather than make statements. They are reluctant to reveal personal information or feelings and use thinking words such as, "I think if you look carefully at the statistics, you'll find that I'm right." They are excellent step-by-step evaluators and fact checkers because they focus mostly on the details and numbers. You may hear them say, "The numbers don't lie. There's no other way to look at this." High Cs make excellent accountants, bookkeepers, data entry technicians, editors, and technical engineers.

Competent Styles are non-contact people who prefer the formality of distance. They'll arrange their desks and chairs for functionality, usually creating a separation between you and their personal space. They are not into hugging and prefer a cool handshake. You'll feel them stiffen if you attempt to get too close. Their gait is usually slow and methodical with a focused effort to reach a known destination.

Mode of Dress

When it comes to a High C's appearance, picture Felix Unger who is noticeably understated and the neat perfectionist on television's *The Odd Couple*. Like Felix, Competent Styles tend to wear more conservative clothes, but with unique, often perfectly matched accessories. They prefer a more understated, perfectly groomed appearance.

Cs thrive on unraveling life's complexities; they may choose jazz or classical rock and enjoy driving well-built, practical cars like Cadillacs or Volvos that perform well in conservative, understated colors like brown, gray, or white.

Voicemail Message Tips for High Cs :

- Articulate clearly at a steady rate of speech

- Remain cool, calm, and professional

- Tell them exactly why you are calling and get to the point quickly

- Tell them exactly what you want them to do without sugar-coating

- Let them know what to expect with the next step

If you are emailing a High C, use this email sales example:

> Monique,
>
> I just read a very informative article about how smart salespeople are systematizing every aspect of their client/prospect communication activities.
>
> You may click here to read an article that teaches how to leverage high-tech sales systems that automate high-touch sales campaigns to add more clients to your database.
>
> I look forward to supporting you in your marketing success.

High Cs tend to be formal so you'll want to address them with "Good afternoon, Mr. Roberts. This is Asha Sawyer. You asked me to call back Monday morning." Formal greetings are a tip-off that you may be dealing with a Competent Style. Competent Styles are time-conscious, dependable individuals who complete a task when they say they will.

Many people in this category call themselves by their given names, not by nicknames. It's Elizabeth, Rebecca, Donald, and Peter, not Beth, Becka, Don, or Pete. Of course, there are exceptions. This type seems less likely to tolerate what they perceive as cute nicknames for themselves, such as Johnny, Ricky, Cindy, or Becky.

Competent styles make perfect virtual assistants because they will take copious notes while being instructed in order to perform requests correctly. They are slow to start, but once they have clarity on the requested task, they will happily repeat it over and over again with perfection.

Do not rush these people in the learning phase of the process to alleviate frustration, fear, and confusion. They are a hard-working reliable part of the team and a visionary's golden ticket to success.

Focus on brief, to-the-point telephone calls. Although they may not tell you to call them Mister or Ms. or Doctor or whatever their titles happen to be, Competent Styles sometimes view jumping into a first-name basis as an invasion of privacy.

They prefer more formal relationships and typically hold their ground in stressful situations with concrete facts or reverse-control questions. They do this quietly and independently, by first avoiding others. Then they take on the problem in an orderly way that aligns with their own carefully formulated plan.

High Cs are inclined to speak in structured, careful speech patterns, almost weighing their words as they say them. They usually ask pertinent questions and talk in a quiet, observant, cautious way. Additionally, they may not volunteer much about their personal lives beyond name, rank, and serial number. "Yes, I'm married with three children. We live in San Francisco." They prefer to keep the relationship formal, yet pleasant and businesslike. Less is more with a Competent Style—less conversation, self-disclosure, and quiet verbal communication keeps them in their comfort zones.

While interacting with a High C, practice your focused listening skills and read between the lines: Detecting longer-than-average silences, especially when asking more personal, private questions, may signal annoyance or reluctance. When this occurs, ask, "Am I getting too personal?" or "If I'm asking uncomfortable questions, could you let me know so I don't make our communication challenging for either of us?"

Competent types may relax more if they think they have an out. They tend to express themselves in a rather tentative manner. "I'll check on that and let you know tomorrow." Or they may want to provide you with information so you can form your own conclusions. "I have a copy of the president's report in my files. If I send it to you, perhaps you'll find what you're looking for." Both of these approaches satisfy a Conscientious' need for caution and correctness. He simply may not want to get misquoted or, possibly, involved in the first place.

Summing Up for Sales

Study the personality types carefully. As you move through your day, interacting with others, practice defining whom you are talking to and give them the respect they are due. You'll be amazed by how this knowledge will support you in moving through a day of ease. With everyone you come in contact, ask yourself first: Is this person a visionary or a step-by-step? Then see whether you can guess which personality he or she is in the DISC style. If you aren't sure, go back and review. It's easiest to start practicing with the people closest to you.

I think you'll find that you will clearly enhance your sales relationships once you have an understanding of how each person wishes to be addressed, and if you took your own DISC Sales profile assessment, you'll be well aware of what floats your boat and why you react to others the way you do. Make your practice fun, and if you get it wrong, who cares. It's time to laugh at your mistakes and chalk them up as a new learning experience.

In the next section, we'll discuss the 3 Step Sales Waltz™ and learn how to open a sales conversation, why the sales techniques that used to work are antiquated, and what the clients we work with today are looking for in your words.

This section also includes the third personality-identifying layer. Now you get to learn the secret for getting client lean-in by speaking the words your clients are waiting to hear. This is the secret to selling authenticity that few, if any, sales courses include, and it's why my students suddenly love sales. No more scripts—woo-hoo!

PART TWO
WALTZING THROUGH SALES

"Words can be like X-rays if you use them properly—they'll go through anything. You read and you're pierced."

— Aldous Huxley, *Brave New World*

♡

CHAPTER 7

The Genius in Your Words

Now that you know the importance of choosing peace in your life, what it means to be DISC-literate, and who you are as a salesperson, it's essential to focus on the words you use while interacting with your clients so they can easily understand the benefits you offer and how you can support them.

My students learn that it's vital to their business to:

- Develop and follow their business blueprint
- Utilize active listening skills
- Speak with good purpose
- Use the benefits and phrases their clients are waiting to hear
- Look deeply within to overcome negativity and fear

SELLING AUTHENTICALLY

One of the biggest challenges I've experienced with business owners is when I begin to speak about heartfelt sales. Right away, entrepreneurs puff up their defenses and say, "Oh, I've been selling for years. I don't need any help with that." And that's the problem. If you've been selling since *The Tonight Show Starring Johnny Carson*, your techniques are obsolete. You've been trained in antiquated methods. The era of ninety-nine nos to get one yes is outdated and ridiculous. It was great back then when we believed that sales was a numbers game, but in today's sales environment, you'll starve. Besides, it's a huge waste of time, so why are coaches and trainers still teaching these antique methods? Can you imagine how much time it takes to connect with ninety-nine people so they can tell you "No"? It hurts the psyche too. Who wants to get rejected that many times? Not me.

In today's sales environment, we focus on the long-term. We build relationships and develop communities that work together to provide referrals for one another. Winners follow the relationship model. It's easier, more authentic, and a very different approach. We no longer focus on manipulation, killer power closes, or sales-y type scripting, and we avoid becoming known as a "one hit wonder," a term used to identify selling one item to one person whom you will never see again.

BREAKING THROUGH THE NOISE

Nowadays, there's a lot of noise out there when it comes to marketing, and most of it we've become immune to or learned to ignore. So how do you break through? Here's the secret: People buy you. They're not interested in fancy brochures, slick sales closes, your company name, sales-y scripts and phrases or whether you're the best in the West.

Research has shown that people are suspicious and fearful of salespeople and their marketing techniques. This means we need to overcome and lower the level of fear our clients experience while trying to make an educated decision.

Here's another consideration: People are basically selfish. Before you get your hackles up, I implore you to think hard about this. Wouldn't you agree that if spending your money on expensive products or services doesn't provide a benefit you need, you probably won't purchase that product? If you said yes, then you're in agreement with the majority of the population. In fact, I don't know anyone who buys something just for the fun of it unless it's movie tickets or for something entertaining. Taking into account that the majority of people are selfish, ask yourself, "What benefits do I provide my clients that fill a need?" You'll find more information about crafting your benefits in Chapter 9.

LISTENING TO YOUR THOUGHTS

Write down what the little voice in your head is saying to you right now about sales. What fears are coming up for you? Take a moment to write down all of your fears and the negative thoughts you're having. You might even write about what experiences you've had with selling your product or service in the past and what fearful feelings were triggered in each experience.

_____

_____

_____

_____

_____

_____

_____

_____

This is an important step because what we say to ourselves is who we become. Sometimes the gremlins in our thoughts torpedo our efforts so much so that they shut us down completely. It's what we say, feel, and believe that keeps us in our prisons of limitation.

Thoughts are things we manifest into reality. I have a friend who constantly says, "This work is killing me." And every time I talk to her, she has another illness even greater than the last. Her words are literally killing her. What are your words doing to you? What are they bringing into your life? Are they increasing your income or depleting your health?

Your intent determines the answer to whether or not you have success in your business. You can literally speak your life and your sales into existence if you are willing to commit to what you want to create. But first you must decide what it is you want.

The best way to begin is to decide first how much money you need every month to pay your bills, and second, how much money you want to make each month to live the lifestyle you deserve. Don't be vague. Write the amount you intend to make monthly on a colorful piece of paper, tape it onto your refrigerator, and look at it every morning. What is that number and how many programs or products do you need to sell in order to hit that number? Maybe your number is $10,000.

This is a great exercise to change how your mind accepts the fact that you will make $10,000 a month. Sometimes, a number like that is hard to wrap your mind around and accept so let's try an exercise that will make it easier for you.

Breathe in deeply, exhale slowly, and then close your eyes. Breathe three more times and exhale to the count of ten. Then say to yourself, "I am making $10,000 every month," and listen to what the little voice in your head tells you in response.

Say it again and listen in. What did it say this time? Repeat "I am making $10,000 every month." Now what did it say? Continue saying the same phrase until your little voice agrees with your goal. Say this phrase five times each time you say it, and say it three times a day, for seven days if you really want to make $10,000 every month. The Law of Attraction says whatever you think, say, and believe is what the Universe will deliver into your experience.

Do not let your little voice take control of your life. You are not that little voice. You are in control, and when you say this statement five times, three times a day, for a week, your little voice will believe you and say, "Yes, you will." If not, keep repeating the phrase until your mind agrees with what you want.

I was just listening to a book on Audible called *Thought Vibration* by William Walker Atkinson. In it, Atkinson agrees with me in saying that thoughts are things and what we think manifests into our lives. The Law of Attraction has a huge effect on our lives and our business income, so let me remind you that you get what you think about. Focus on your intent and not what you lack.

With persistent intent and positive thoughts, you will surely succeed in anything you wish to accomplish. But you must become aware of that little voice in your head and the words you say out loud that counter your efforts. When you catch yourself thinking or saying something negative, instantly replace it with the words "Cancel. Cancel. Cancel," and then make a positive statement over and over again until your mind says, "Okay, I get it." Get out of the habit of victimhood and come into the world of positive abundance.

In the next chapter, we'll work on defining your target market sweet spot. This is a very important step in your business blueprint and imperative for generating a consistent income. Even though you might think you can sell to everyone, you can't, and thinking so is probably why you are having such a hard time making sales while you run from one networking group to the next and feel burnt out.

"Success doesn't necessarily come from breakthrough innovation but from flawless execution. A great strategy alone won't win a game or a battle; the win comes from basic blocking and tackling."

— Naveen Jain

♡

CHAPTER 8

Defining Your Target Market

Establishing your target market ensures that your messaging will resonate with clients who have the need or desire for your skills or product. This important step has a major impact on the stability of your business and increasing sales.

Defining your target market, demographic, perfect customer, or customer avatar—it really doesn't matter what you call your target market; all four descriptions mean the same thing. They refer to the people who fit into your programs, products, or services perfectly. These are the clients looking for you who can afford what you're selling.

Please don't tell me your target market is everyone or anyone who wants what you've got. If that's your belief, then that's why your sales aren't soaring. It's simply not possible to speak to everyone because people speak different lifestyle languages.

Think about who might be looking for you and who might need the benefits you offer in your professional area of expertise. Some business owners say they sell to anyone who needs what they're peddling, but that's almost impossible, and it's a very slow way to generate an income. If you attempt to sell to everyone, no one will hear you. My target market is solopreneurs and small business owners between the ages of forty-five and sixty-five, who are struggling with sales, feeling pushy, fearing rejection, and generally don't feel good about asking for money. They probably don't know how to assemble programs for ease of selling, have no outlined business blueprint, and have no knowledge of how to create an engaging phraseology to attract their clients.

According to Bloomberg, this situation describes 98 percent of entrepreneurs. That's a huge market, so fortunately, I don't have to look too hard to find them. If you haven't pinpointed your target market, think about industries or areas you could work in that have a high percentage of people who need you.

I witnessed this just yesterday at an event I attended here in San Diego. A woman was chasing certification after certification in the Ayurveda medicine field and was talking about teaching classes, but when I asked her why she had chosen to do this specific business and what her intention was, she became annoyed with me for asking. "I'm not making a plan. I'm just going with what shows up," she said, indicating to me, and those sitting around the table, that she had no idea what she was doing.

An attitude and behavior like this is exactly why a high percentage of businesses go under. If you're serious about your business, the steps I'll walk you through in these pages will keep you in the 20 percent who thrive. But remember, first, you must know who your target market is; otherwise, your clients will never find you.

No one can sell everyone at the same time. Even the largest corporations target their marketing campaigns to a specific demographic. If they didn't, no one would buy their products because the verbiage would be incorrect and confusing to their prospective purchasers. If you think I'm kidding, watch the commercials on TV. See whether you can determine whom they are directing their ad campaign toward. Notice, I said to see whether you can determine to whom the ad is directed. I didn't say we always are able to figure out what the ad is selling.

If you want to thrive in business, you must determine whom you want to work with and never waver from your decision. If you choose incorrectly or skip this step, you will probably fail.

Deciding exactly whom you wish to market to, speak to, and focus on is an entrepreneur's most difficult challenge, and it is perhaps one of the biggest reasons why entrepreneurs give up and go back to their day jobs. I can't begin to tell you how many business owners tell me that everyone is her client. That's a myth that will drive you out of business fast!

All of your future income and business success hinges on this one carefully thought-out decision. Here is where you need a great coach who can help you see who will most benefit from your talents, programs, and goals. A golden mistake in this process will be so much more than the cost of a coach. It will be the demise of your business and your entrepreneurial dreams.

All of your marketing materials, interviews, social media activity, and networking efforts must be directed toward this one target audience. Every opportunity to show up must fit into this demographic or you're wasting your time. Time is money, so once you determine whom your target market is, it's imperative that you remain tightly focused and avoid all distractions or deviations from the market you've chosen.

This doesn't mean that you can't work with people outside of your defined target market. It simply means that these are the people you target, so all of your marketing materials and verbiage are directed toward your chosen demographic.

If you've been in business for a year, think about who has been interested in your products or service. Who is the easiest demographic to talk to when discussing what it is you have to offer? Who has shown an interest? Why was he or she interested?

Recently, I had a discussion with one of my clients. She works with individuals who want to produce the feeling of joy in their lives. For years, she spent tens of thousands of dollars attempting to sell entrepreneurs similar to my own target market. Just recently, she determined that she was not working with a target market that could afford to buy her retreats and services because the people in that market were too focused on funding their businesses' development.

The reality is that no money is budgeted by entrepreneurs for bringing the feeling of joy into their lives. After five years of lost time and income, she has changed her target market to women over sixty, who are not in business, and who may be widows or divorced. This is an entirely different demographic and more suitable to her specialty.

Another client wanted to work with millennials, educating them on how to build a successful business. During our discussion, he determined that because millennials are raising their families and working as employees, they do not have enough additional money left in the household budget to pay for his services.

DETERMINING YOUR OWN TARGET MARKET

Here are some important considerations to think about while determining your target market.

Under the age of twenty-five, people are still focusing on a career, getting out of college, getting a job, and beginning their families. Few have enough life experience or maturity to run a business. Many are still living at home with Mom and Dad and may still be reeling from college debt. This is not a great target market unless you are in the business of selling cars or essential oils.

Between the ages of twenty-five and forty-five, people are raising families, working as employees, and budgeting pretty tightly while saving for their kids' college educations, caring for their parents, and providing for their financial futures. We call these people the "sandwich generation" because they're stuck in the middle of providing financial assistance in so many different directions. Most have very little time or additional money to spend on anything other than supporting their families.

Between the ages of forty-five and sixty-five, people may be divorced, widowed, laid off from a job they've given fifteen years to, or in the painful process of reinventing themselves. They may be just finishing up with paying college tuitions, so now there is spare money to start their own businesses, take advantage of traveling opportunities, and participate in events and programs they enjoy. Often, they're most concerned with their health, exercise, travel, or a new business launch that speaks to their souls.

Now it's your turn to decide whom you can best serve. Whom do you feel comfortable working with and why? Understand that this decision isn't cut in stone. You may find out later that you need to revise your choice just like my clients revised theirs. Sometimes, we don't know for sure whether we've chosen the correct target market until we test it. This is what I mean by tacking back and forth, testing the market and not trying to sell, before you can zero in on your perfect target market.

Answer these questions:

Do you want to work with entrepreneurs or employees? Speaking to employees requires a very different language from the words and phrases we use when speaking to entrepreneurs.

_____

_____

What is the age range that you believe best suits your product or service and why?

_____

_____

_____

What three primary interests do the people in your target market have or enjoy? This question supports you in determining whether your programs are priced correctly. You may find that your chosen target market may not be able to afford your products on a monthly basis. Mentioning these primary interests in your marketing and interview opportunities draws your clients toward you.

_____

_____

_____

Do they have families with children at home? If so, what are their ages? If you are marketing to families, you'll want to know the average age range of the children. If you are a realtor or mortgage lender, this would be a good thing to know. Families don't often move during the school year and may live in their homes for up to seven to ten years.

_____

_____

_____

Which would be more suitable for you to work with—women, men, or both, and why? (Hint: Keep in mind that men and women have different languages, so you'd need to tailor your speeches to meet the needs of both, which is much harder but still doable.)

_____

_____

Write out a full tightly worded statement of whom you intend to serve and why this is the best target market for your product or service.

_____

_____

_____

Finally, before speaking anywhere, find out whether the people attending the event are within your demographic/target market and how many participants are expected to attend. This will save you a great deal of time and frustration unless you simply want this time as a practice session. Speaking to the wrong demographic will only frustrate and disappoint you because there will be no response to the massive amount of energy you put out in an effort to connect with your audience.

In the next chapter, you'll learn better ways to define your perfect target market with some much-needed secret sauce.

"If you really care about humanity you are going to want to meet their needs and fulfill something in their lives. When we make a difference in people's lives we get fulfilled. You have to care about people and find out what they really need."

— Dr. John Demartini

♡

CHAPTER 9

Pouring on the Secret Sauce

On June 6, 2017, Dr. John Demartini was on my syndicated radio show, *Ascended Masters at Work*. In his quote on the opposite page, he was responding to a question about the importance of finding out your target market's wants and needs before you spend hours creating programs and attempting to sell products, or years writing a book.

If we don't care enough and take the time to interact with our target market, then speaking on stages, networking, and doing radio and televisions interviews will not be a success. Many times, we don't get sales because: 1) people in our target market aren't aware that they need what we're selling, 2) we haven't built enough trust with them, 3) they don't know enough about our product or service to be convinced that it's right for them, 4) we haven't made the effort to find out why a client might need us to formulate our program around that need, or 5) we haven't built up a consistency of awareness so people have no idea who we are and cannot trust our credibility. We'll discuss this further in the massive visibility section of this book.

Remember, you know who you are, what you've accomplished in your career, and why you're the best fit for the job, but your prospects know nothing about you except what the presenter read from your bio.

You can quickly overcome prospect connection disadvantages by speaking your clients' perfect words and phrases. This will draw them toward you, and it creates an instant connection with the specific people in your audience who will resonate with your words. Herein lies the corporate secret to easing in a transition of trust and connection between you and your perfect clients.

TESTING YOUR TARGET MARKET

The best way to relate and test your target market is to do research. Come on; there's no reason to groan and moan about this. Actually, it can be a lot of fun, and you might even get a few unexpected clients. A few steps are needed to accomplish this goal, but in the long run, they pay very well. The ultimate goal is to get on the phone or out in the field and ask twenty very well-defined interview questions that relate to what you are selling. (I'll give you some examples in the next section.) How well your interview questions are developed is the determiner for how easily you'll be able to make sales in the future.

The step-by-step High Cs excel in this project, and you can visibly see them move forward rapidly. High D visionaries think they already know it all and are quick to look for a step-by-step person to do it for them. They frequently put up a resistance until they see the benefits the High Cs receive and then their competitive natures spur them forward. High Ss maintain that slow steady pace while agonizing over constructing the questions and setting appointments to accomplish the task. This pace is painful to watch, and during our sales boot camp calls, I'm constantly moving them forward with gentle support and encouragement. High Is have no problem taking the steps necessary to meet their goals and sometimes decide to make it a game. In any case, move through this process quickly if you want to benefit your clients and make money quickly. Overall, the High Cs and the High Is tend to move through this assignment the fastest, and they learn amazing things about what they thought their clients wanted or needed compared to the reality of their discoveries.

Some of my students do an awesome job with this task and get new clients in the process; others I'll remind over and over again until they'll finally complete it; and then there are those who do everything they can to avoid the process completely. Those who avoid it are the ones who are left behind and suffer financially.

Here is the step-by-step process, but remember, your questions are the key, and the wrong questions won't get you to the Promised Land. Think carefully, and if necessary, get support sooner rather than later.

POURING ON THE SECRET SAUCE

Rule 1

Determine twenty questions that relate specifically to your business.

Start with the easy questions. I've provided the first six questions for you. It's not required that you use these specific questions, but come up with ones that you think will work for your situation, your defined target market, and your interview opportunity. These questions simply make it easier for you to start the interview process.

1. **Do you have children and what are their ages?**

    If your demographic has young children, you want to include comments in your speaking opportunities that talk about young children and their relationship to your topic, or simply tell a quick little story about an experience with a child and how it relates to your topic in your speeches.

2. **What type of car do you drive, what year is it, and what do you love or dislike about it?**

   Learning this information helps you relate to your audience. If many of the people you interview say they drive a Volvo because it's a tank and has a great accident protection rating to keep their children safe, you want to include that in your interviews and speeches by saying something like, "You know how it is when you're driving in all that traffic. There's nothing like a Volvo to protect the kids."

   If you sell insurance, you might say something like, "Life insurance is a great protection for your family just like a Volvo's safety approval rating. I know you know what I mean." Your perfect client will then think, "I know exactly what she means. She gets me." With this technique, you're building a relationship, familiarity, and trust. Using a phrase like this literally calls your client to you.

3. **Do you work? What do you like about your job? What do you dislike?**

   Learning and using this information brings you a step closer to connecting with the perfect clients in your audience. With this question, you find out what your prospects love about their work, what they dislike, and you'll also determine whether the majority of the people you're interviewing are entrepreneurs or employees.

   In this example, we'll say they are employees. What most of them dislike about their jobs is the drive to and from work in the traffic. What they love about their jobs are the friendships created with coworkers.

   If I'm speaking on a stage or giving a radio interview, in my role as financial educator, this information is very important. I could say, "I know you love your work and the relationships you've built with your coworkers, but that hour of driving to and from work in traffic must be very painful. Working as an employee puts you in the highest tax bracket, but what if I could show you a way to reduce your taxes and keep more money in your pocket?"

This question gives your prospects the idea that they don't know what they don't know. They'll wonder, *How could I save on taxes?* It's simply a seed that you plant in their heads that makes them want to follow up with you and learn more.

4. **Do you own a home and how long have you lived there?**

If most of the clients in your target market own a home and move often, it would be a big factor to consider if you are a real estate agent, lender, home decorator, landscape architect, kitchen remodeler, or carpet or window-covering salesperson.

If your clients, on average, own homes for only three to five years, they'll be your clients forever if you provide great service because you'll work with them every three to five years in their new homes. Can you see the importance of these questions and how they affect the way you do business?

If you do home decor or landscaping and you find out your perfect clients primarily live in apartments or have been living in their homes for forty years, you'll have a difficult time making money and need to consider changing your target market.

This formula is a quick way to identify the group of people you want to work with so you can revise your decision if you find out you're targeting the wrong market. But how will you know if you don't take this important step with diligence? Why not let people know you care enough about them to ask them what they want and then show them you can make a difference in their lives?

Here's an example: One of my students is in her seventies. She works with people who go through difficult changes in their lives such as job loss, loss of a loved one, or divorce.

For years, she had been marketing her program to her own demographic. During this exercise, she determined that people in their late sixties and seventies don't normally work and are enjoying their retirement. This eliminated the job loss coaching, which was one-third of her business strategy. Her perfect clients also weren't experiencing divorce because they weren't married. Their husbands had already died or they were divorced twelve or more years prior. This left only grief counseling, but she didn't want to focus on grief. Obviously, because of this exercise, my student decided to change her demographic to women in their forties to early sixties because two-thirds of her planned demographic didn't need her services.

5. **What is your favorite color?**

Provide five pre-selected colors and ask your clients to rate their top three favorite colors. The color that is rated third best is your accent color and the other two colors are your primary branding colors.

What colors are your perfect clients attracted to? Once you determine this, you'll know what colors to include in your marketing materials and handouts. This question, again, brings you and your clients closer because they can easily relate and identify with your color scheme. Don't choose your own colors. If you're a woman and fuchsia is your color but you're working with all men, you might want to choose blue.

6. **Do you enjoy traveling? What is your favorite vacation or adventure spot, and what's on the top of your bucket list?**

This question gives you a great idea about how much money people in your potential target market have. If they travel a great deal, you know their coffers are deep and there's money to spend. A student in my last class found out that the majority of her clients resonate with Sedona. Now, to call in her perfect client, she finds ways to weave Sedona into her speeches and she plans retreats there.

Now you have six of the twenty interview questions. Find a quiet space and work on the remaining fourteen questions that relate to your business. What do you want to know about your clients? Write down your questions below.

7. _____

_____

8. _____

_____

9. _____

_____

10. _____

_____

11. _____

_____

12. _____

_____

13. _____

_____

14. _____

_____

15. _____

_____

16. _____

_____

17. _____

_____

18. _____

_____

19. _____

_____

20. _____

_____

Rule 2

You must be focused on interviewing only those who fit into your target market. Do not waste your time interviewing friends and family unless they fit into your specific demographic.

Rule 3

Set up a free conference calling account and record all of your interviews so you can relax, enjoy, and interact with your clients' responses. Do not try to take notes while conducting your interviews. Remember to be an active listener, asking really great questions while showing an interest in your clients' responses. Tell your clients to call into the number and give them the code. Don't forget to hit the record button!

Rule 4

Set up three appointments per day. Let your interviewees know that it will take approximately twenty minutes to complete your interview questions and that you'd be happy to share the results with them when the interviews have been completed. Some will be excited about this opportunity and some won't. If the call runs long, ask permission to continue at the end of the twenty-minute mark.

Rule 5

Turn on the recording button and begin your conversations with, "If it's okay with you, I'll be recording this interview so I can focus on the importance of what you are sharing. Are you in agreement?" Make sure each client agrees at the beginning of the interview recording. Then have each one state his or her name, age, and city of residence.

Rule 6

Review your recordings. Transcribe each call. If you don't want to do it yourself, hire someone at Fiverr.com for a nominal fee. He or she can do the hard work for you, but it's your job to listen carefully to each person's emotional expression. People will express their deepest beliefs by enunciating with emotion.

Rule 7

Extract the specific words and phrases out of each answer and then compare to see how often they're used. Use these words and phrases in everything you do, including your marketing, introducing yourself at networking events, on your thirty-second promo, on the stage, and during one-on-one conversations.

Rule 8

Now that you have the frequently used phrases to incorporate into your vocabulary, determine the ten most frequently used words that describe the pain your product or service is there to solve. Learn these specific words and phrases, and use them at every opportunity.

Rule 9

Follow up with your interviewees to give them the results and listen to their thoughts.

You now have the secret sauce that every corporation and every entrepreneur should utilize to speak the words and phrases that will get your clients' attention on any marketing piece, stage, radio, podcast, or web TV interview.

CRAFTING YOUR BENEFITS INTO WORDS

One of the most important steps, aside from defining your target market and understanding who you are and how to work with others, is gaining clarity on the benefits you offer your clients. Think about what your benefits are and see whether you can list them in short succinct sentences.

Over the years, I've noticed that when business owners attempt to sell, they get caught up in the systems of how they perform whatever the product or service is. They don't understand that the client is only looking for the program's benefits. In Chapter 9, we'll look into this concept further and learn how to deliver your benefits in a way that your clients will hear and understand. Then they'll be willing to take the next step and buy from you.

Here are three examples of the benefits I offer my students and how I verbalize them:

1. Entrepreneurs appreciate learning how to sell authentically so they can show up massively and make a much bigger income. In order to thrive, we need to get out of our own backyards.

2. Developing programs that sell easily and pricing them correctly creates a consistent monthly income that you can depend on.

3. Learning how to sell authentically, without scripts, makes it easy to open sales conversations and develop lifelong referral relationships with your clients.

Benefits Exercise

Now it's your turn to write three benefit statements that will entice your clients and solve their problems or challenges. Do not bypass this step. Think carefully about why someone would want to buy from you. What is it that 98 percent of the people in your target market, in your specialized area of expertise, want and need? Even if they don't know they need your product or program specifically, they'll understand your benefit statement and think, "Aha, that's exactly what I need."

Benefit Statement 1:

_____

_____

Benefit Statement 2:

_____

_____

Benefit Statement 3:

_____

_____

If you are struggling to answer this question, watch a few TV commercials. They've got this technique down perfectly so you can learn a lot by watching how they suck people in. The car ads are some of the best. The shopping networks have this down really well too. As you watch, write down what you liked about each commercial's approach, the words it used to get people's interest, and the age group you think it is marketing toward.

Now think about what you offer. What do you offer and why would someone want it? Name the desired point you want to make, and then provide the benefit.

Next, figure out what the phrases are that create the benefit statements your clients are looking for. If you dig deeply into my benefit statements, you'll find the phrases that define the benefits I offer.

Here are the benefits I offer my clients who are looking for the solutions to sales:

- Learn the 3 Step Sales Waltz™ to Sales Success. (Sales success)

- Zero in on Your Perfect Clients and Draw Them Toward You. (Determine your target market)

- Easily Overcome Objections, Rejection, and Feeling Pushy. (Overcome the pain of rejection)

- Speak the Words Your Clients Are Waiting to Hear for Quicker Connections. (Quicker connections)

- Discover How to Open a Sales Conversation Easily.

- Learn the Secret to Caring Client Retention. (Keep your clients buying)

- Profile Yourself as a Salesperson and Acquire the Art of Engaging with Heart. (Find out who you are and how to relate to your clients.)

- Engage Confidently and Authentically in the Sales Process Without Scripts. (Sell authentically.)

- Attend Ninety-Day Weekly Group Coaching Sales Boot Camp for easier sales conversions (make money)

Now that you've had some time to review my list of benefits, see whether you can list five benefits, including the three you listed above, by indicating what it is your clients receive while working with you and how it benefits them. Put each benefit into a sentence that will call in your clients. Give it a try. How could you word your benefits to call in your clients?

1. _____

_____

_____

2. _____

_____

_____

3. _____

_____

_____

4. _____

_____

_____

5. _____

_____

_____

In the next chapter, we move to Layer 3 and learn how to use the words and phrases that our clients are waiting to hear, but it's very important that you complete the Secret Sauce exercise before moving forward or the next chapter may not make much sense. The words and phrases needed for the next chapter exercise will come directly from the interview questions and are encased in what, how, and why phrases. You'll also learn how to paint the dream in "what if" sentences that entice your clients. For example:

"What if I could show you how to speak to your clients in a way that made them want to contact you rather than you calling them?"

"Pretend that every single person you meet has a sign around his or her neck that says, 'Make me feel important.' Not only will you succeed in sales, you will succeed in life."

— Mary Kay Ash

♡

CHAPTER 10

Delivering Four-Point Information Phrases

Delivering four-point information phrases is how we speak with good purpose to both the big picture and the step-by-step people. We went over the identification of these designations in Chapter 4. While speaking on stage, interviewing on radio, or sitting with a host on a TV show, you will always need to address the four types of information your clients are waiting to hear.

Here's what I mean: Everyone we work with focuses on getting the answers to one or more of these questions when confronted with a new idea: "Why would I want to pay for this product or service?" or "What is this product or service (details)?" or "How would I use this product or service effectively?" Which question do you ask? I'm a big picture-how person and a High I. If you tell me what the product or service is, I'm going to want to know how it will effectively work into my needs. What perplexes me most is sitting in a seminar where a coach rambles on about what I'm supposed to do, be, or have in my business, but I have no idea how to put it into effect and make it work for my business. That's why I've made such a big effort in this book to give you the how instead of just telling you what you need to do and why you need to do it.

I've provided more information about how each of these processes works, and below I've provided the words and phrases I use to add clarity. You will also have an opportunity to write your own phrases to satisfy each person in your audience who is reading your marketing messages.

Keep in mind that there are some people who can't figure out why they'd need your product or service and they're waiting for that answer, while others like High Cs want to know not only what it is but what the details are and why it works.

WORDING FOR WHY, WHAT, AND HOW

Why People: These people want lots of benefits and more benefits. The best way to address this desire is by making a point and then providing a clear benefit.

Here's an example I use for the Massive Visibility Media™ course:

Point: Creating your own professional home studio…

Benefit: Creating a home video saves thousands of dollars on video production because you can do it all for free in front of your computer.

Here's an example for the Celebrity Guest Expert TV Training.

Point: Discover the answers for how to become a "Go-To" Celebrity Guest Expert.

Benefit: Get the secrets for showing up professionally with confidence on radio, podcasts, web TV, and stages.

Write one "why" statement that your clients will find irresistible. Remember to include the benefits you created at the end of Chapter 9. These are the answers for why your clients want to work with you.

Write Your Why Statement

_____

_____

_____

What People: These people want the answers for what you are selling. The "what" is not your system for how your clients get to your benefits unless they are High Cs. High Cs want all of the details about everything, and they won't buy until they've done their research. It's best to give them time to root through all of the data without pushing.

What you can say is, "In this course, you'll do this, then that, and then this, and then, voilà!"

Here's what I say to my potential "what" students:

"I teach massive visibility for massive income so you can get outside your own backyard and make an impact that makes a big difference in your income. If you've been running from one networking group to the next and find that the money just isn't there, you might be ready to make a bigger impact. Have you experienced that?"

Now it's your turn to write a "what" statement that will call in your clients:

(Hint: Try writing this sentence without the words "I help.")

My What Statement

_____

How People: The "how" people want experiential and detailed steps for where they want to go. It you don't offer enough clarity, they say, "I'm confused." These people want details that lead to results. If you can show them exactly how to get where they want to go, they will be your clients for life. They will also be an awesome mouthpiece for testimonials and give you great referrals.

What I say is:

"First, we start with my course Compel Don't Sell, and you learn the DISC Sales process and how to relate to and build relationships with your clients along with step-by-step techniques for easy sales.

"Then you move into the Business Mastery Platinum course, create three programs, determine the pricing, and develop your marketing blueprint.

"After you've built up your confidence, learned how to sell, and are ready to put clients into your classes, it's time to move into the Massive Visibility Media™ course. Here you construct your own 4x4 video set; create two-minute videos; interview on radio, web TV, podcasts, and webinars; and speak on stages. If you'd like to know more, watch the student testimonials on my Compel Don't Sell course web page at ShirleneReeves.com.

Refine your "how" into three steps that are easy to understand and provide lots of benefits. Give your prospective clients your website sales/landing page address so they can do more research.

Write your three-step experiential exercise for your "how" people:

Experiential Step 1

_____

_____

_____

Experiential Step 2

_____

_____

_____

Experiential Step 3

_____

_____

_____

What If: "What if" statements work for everyone. This is an opportunity to paint the dream of what your product or service provides. Here you fall back on the assignment above and are talking about your benefits. "What if" statements are my favorite, and I use them at least twice in every interview or speech.

Examples:

The first two "what if" examples I will give you are for my media course. The last two I use for my financial clients.

Media

- What if people said to you, like they say to me, "I see you everywhere. How do you do it?"
- What if you could stay at home and shine your light brightly, from your own home studio, and your perfect clients could find you rather than you running yourself into exhaustion with little or no results?

Finance

- What if every man had to come back after he died to see the mess he left for his family because he had no life insurance?
- What if you're losing money you didn't know you were losing?

Now you try it. Write three "what if" statements that would cause your clients to dream about the benefits you provide. You can cheat by looking at your answers to your earlier benefits exercise.

What If:

_____

_____

What If:

_____

_____

What If:

_____

_____

"No one limits your growth but you. If you want to earn more, learn more. That means you'll work harder for a while; that means you'll work longer for a while. But you'll be paid for your extra effort with enhanced earnings down the road."

— Tom Hopkins

♡

CHAPTER 11

Overcoming Sales Fears and Rejection

The fear and anxiety that surfaces around sales can paralyze and doom your business. Many entrepreneurs are afraid of sales but instinctually believe that bringing their mission and their message to the world is why they are participating here in Earth School. They push themselves so hard that they become ill, overworked, and physically hit bottom, no longer able to run.

Many others, who have enough modalities, credentials, knowledge, and experience to paper the walls, are searching for the answer to who they are, and they have no idea how to blend everything they know and do into one business. Members of this group usually have searched for years and spent thousands of dollars looking for the answer to one most important question: "With everything I know, how do I say what I do?"

This question is the platform for the next step in your business success. Without this answer, you will feel paralyzed with fear. After all, how can you sell what you do without the answers for who you are as a business?

Two clients recently came to me with one baseline question, "I know so much that I don't know where to begin. Every time someone asks me what I do, a wave of fear washes over me and I don't know what to say." One client had already spent over $10,000 on her quest, with no results. The other had been working with two coaches for six months, but she still hadn't found her answer.

Both clients were about to give up when we started working together. It took no longer than two hours of one-on-one work to discover and create each one's Business Identity. Today, they feel a sense of peace and excitement while stepping forward confidently into positioning their business and interacting with potential clients.

These and many other clients say that now when potential clients ask them what they do, it's easy to explain their business identity succinctly and confidently while putting their new relationship development into practice.

Stedman Graham trains individuals and organizations to maximize their potential by developing strong identities. In his talk during Youth Success Week 2016 in Oceanside, California, he said, "We live in a skill-based age, and if not constantly learning and innovating, we become obsolete." He went on to say that, "If you don't know what to do with your mind, others will control your time."

It's important that you are always moving forward toward overcoming your fears and challenges. It's not difficult if you bite off small chunks and tack back and forth taking one step at a time toward your intended goal. That way you will purposely build the skills you need the most and relate to the least.

Sales expertise is one of an entrepreneur's most necessary skills, but it seems to raise the most fear and anxiety. Once you have answers and begin evolving into your business identity, it's time to begin thinking about how to make money.

The challenge is that there is a great divide between knowing what our mission is and the developed skill of sharing that information, service, or product with others who don't even know they need it. Herein lies the dividing line between those who remain in business and those who become obsolete. Communication is key to supporting your clients in understanding your message and defining a target market that is looking for what you provide.

Clarity in your message supports you in the process of breaking through when speaking to your prospects. Time and again, I've witnessed business owners rambling on in lengthy explanations when asked what they do. Have you noticed this? After about the third sentence, the prospect has already lost interest and is looking for an opening for escape.

There are two challenges to take into consideration if you want to overcome the effects of runaway clients:

1. Evaluate the clarity of your explanations.

2. Formulate a Plan.

Challenge 1 is what we've been talking about so far throughout this book. You need to describe succinctly the benefits you provide and only use five to seven words to define the product or service you are selling.

Once you've accomplished this challenge, formulate a plan to reach your target audience. In a perfect world, 98 percent of the people in your target market will need your product or service. Here's an example of what I mean: I work in the world of entrepreneurs, and 98 percent of them are either using outdated sales techniques or aren't aware of how to sell at all. This means I have an airtight target market with a great many potential clients.

Since we've already explored Challenge 1 in previous chapters, let's focus now on Challenge 2.

CHALLENGE 2: FORMULATING A PLAN

Entrepreneurs and coaches don't take into consideration that a marketing and sales blueprint is important for developing and implementing their sales skills. Frequently, the plan is either incomplete or entrepreneurs have a plan, but they aren't clear about how to implement it. As I said before, we don't plan to fail. We simply fail to plan. I believe that this is why Bloomberg consistently reports that 80 percent of businesses fail every year.

A great many entrepreneurs put the cart before the horse. They're so anxious to sprint out of the chute and start networking that they forget to learn the important sales and marketing skills considered to be the glue that holds their business together. Without sales expertise, an entrepreneur is doomed to fail.

"I hate sales," many entrepreneurs tell me. "I don't want to be pushy, and most of all, I don't like rejection. It hurts my feelings when my friends tell me no, and sometimes, I see some of them hide out so they don't have to talk to me. I just don't understand. I have a really great product. Aside from that, it's hard to ask for the money. If I'm honest about it, I really don't have the confidence to sell, and no one taught me how."

"No one?" I ask.

"Well, I went to a sales class this one time, but they gave me scripts and told me I had to produce results. I don't like scripts because they make me feel like I'm not authentic, and if someone asks me a question, or objects to what I'm selling, I don't know what to say."

Some business owners choose to use memorized scripts that don't work because they can't relate to the words in the scripts as their own. Some business owners are pushy and are seen repeatedly asking for the sale until potential clients hide out when they see them coming. Some give glorious descriptions of what they do, but they are afraid of asking for money because they don't know how to handle objections.

Some don't even try to sell because they fear rejection or because when they're asked what they do, they go into stun mode, not knowing how to explain it.

Have you ever heard these types of comments in your circles? Are these comments you might have said yourself? We'll be addressing each of these categories of resistance. Yes, resistance! I thought this would be a great place to begin.

Typically, resistance isn't recognized as a sales challenge. That is why I believe it's important to address it now, and here's how:

1. Begin by allowing yourself to feel what comes up for you while thinking about the sales process. What is it you actually fear, and what are you protecting? What is that tiny voice screaming out in your subconscious saying?

2. The next step is to be okay with your emotional reaction. Talk to your coach or someone you trust about how you feel and where you think this feeling might have come from. Expressing your feelings is a healthy step to overcoming your resistance and fear.

3. Once you've expressed your feelings, see whether you can reframe them into a positive learning experience that will move you toward change and acceptance. Reframing is seeing the current situation from a different perspective. It's a way to move on from a situation in which you feel stuck or confused. Many times, merely reframing one's perspective around the fear and resistance can also change how you feel about the experience that might have triggered your fears.

4. Write everything down in your journal. Your thoughts will become much less intimidating and scary when they're no

longer taking over your mind. Sometimes there is no basis for your fears and they simply arise because you don't have clarity around how to resolve and overcome the anxiety they create. In the later chapters, you will shift from fear and anxiety around the sales process to clarity and confidence.

5. Write down what the difference in outcomes will be in your business when you overcome your resistance and fear of sales.

_____

_____

_____

6. Study what you have written, knowing that all of the positive outcomes you considered are definitely possible. Identify and focus on those most likely to happen and let go of the far-fetched concerns for now.

7. Envision yourself living in the new outcomes you have created and let go of the rest. There is no point in wasting any more energy on something you cannot do anything about. Make a transition plan that takes into consideration all of your options, your support systems, and your behavioral responses to the new change.

REJECTING THE FEAR

Most small business owners fear rejection more than any part of the sales process. It hurts our feelings when our friends and family turn us down or hide out in an attempt to avoid eye contact for fear of being pressured into a sale.

Clients come to me frequently saying, "I was asked to coffee the other day by a new friend. I was really excited that this person cared enough to take the time to get to know me, but then I found out that all he wanted to do was sell to me. It wasn't about becoming friends at all, and now I'll never work with that person. I couldn't get out of there fast enough." Okay, I embellished a bit, but you get the idea.

In the new friend's defense, this person might have been confused about how to open a sales conversation with heart. There aren't many coaches who know how to teach this practice, so be forgiving; maybe someday you'll even have an opportunity to share with that person what you are learning in this book. In any case, I'm sure the person didn't intend to hurt your feelings and make you feel pressured.

There's an art to building relationships into sales. If you do it correctly, your clients will call you and ask for your support instead of you chasing and pressuring them into a sale. Hammering on people to buy from you is a sure way to ruin friendships and wind up lonely, broke, and out of business.

Building relationships before sales will change the dynamics of your friendships, sales, and referral relationships. Get to know people with love in your heart, show a genuine interest, and foster great referral connections. You can easily overcome rejection by building meaningful relationships prior to mentioning what you do in business.

Many times the first step begins at a networking group, an event, on stage, or during a free teleseminar. It's what you say and how you say it. If you approach others, prepared with questions that show you care about their wellbeing, it makes a huge difference in how they perceive you right from the start.

SEEING REJECTION THROUGH YOUR CLIENT'S EYES

No one wants to reject you. They don't do it intentionally to be mean and hurt your feelings. They simply see things through a different pair of binoculars. Early in this book, I mentioned that we all see things differently and that how we choose to see rejection creates peace or pain in our lives, our business, and our minds.

Have you ever felt the pressure of someone so focused on a sale, and needy for her next dollar that she didn't even take the time to get to know you before talking about her amazing service or product? It doesn't feel good, does it? I've noticed that this happens a lot on LinkedIn. Almost as soon as I click the accept button to connect with someone, the person sends me a message like this trying to sell me something:

> Hey, Shirlene, it's great to connect. Here is my story about staying up all night with my Marine mechanics working on changing an F-18 engine in the cold. You have people that are under your leadership, and you realize that you don't know what makes them tick. Maybe you can relate. Go to blah blah blah.com.

Why would I care about a mechanic working on changing an F-18 engine in the cold? Yawn! Who cares? Messages like this irritate the shit out of me. Obviously, this person hasn't even taken the time to look at my LinkedIn profile or he'd know that an article such as this wouldn't interest me. I wonder whether he heard the sound of me disconnecting him. Probably not because there's no one home.

Obviously, some coach, with very little experience, told this marine mechanic that sending out blanket messages to everyone who connects with him on LinkedIn is the answer to making sales. What do you think? How would you respond?

I liken this experience to a coffee date, with a person sitting across from you who is gazing out the window or looking around the room while you're trying to get to know him. I hate to admit it, but

I've been on dates like this. What are these people thinking?

This is exactly why it's imperative to practice active listening skills, ask questions that make your prospect feel heard and understood, and focus only on him during that first meeting. Everyone wants to feel heard and understood. Your clients want to feel that you care enough to hear them. Listening is the answer to building a trusted bond between you.

SHUTDOWNS BY FRIENDS AND FAMILY

Many entrepreneurs run to friends and family when they start a new business and quickly get shut down. Their friends and family members doubt they have the skills or know-how to run a business, much less provide them with a service they want or need. Case in point, if I try to tell my son about something important from a financial perspective, he'll run to the computer and look it up to see whether I'm right. Talk about a High C! He would rather believe the minimal research he finds on the Internet than listen to his mom who has twenty-eight years of training in the financial field. It stymies me that he'd believe someone he doesn't know and who probably doesn't have the credentials and qualifications I've earned and been credited for over so many years.

I tell you this story because I want you to realize that this credibility rejection doesn't only happen to you. My father won't listen to me either because he isn't able to see me as being any older than sixteen. How could a sixteen-year-old know anything? Are you catching my drift? Family and friends have been with you through all of your ups and downs in life, so it's almost impossible for them to view you in a light that makes you a credible and knowledgeable advisor.

The bottom line is stay away from family and friends. They will almost always reject you, and if they do take your advice and something goes wrong down the road, you will be blamed. What do you want—peace or pain? You already know I always choose peace. Don't be concerned about friends and family. Let them learn their own golden lessons. Next!

Fear causes procrastination and stirs up anxiety. Have you ever noticed that when you're supposed to be making sales calls, you suddenly remember the dog needs walking, the laundry hasn't been done, and the house needs cleaning? Next thing you know, you've got the vacuum out and the time for sales calls quickly dwindles into the past. But it doesn't have to be this way. We can get past our fear of rejection.

IDENTIFYING FEAR AND ANXIETY

Anxietycenter.com defines anxiety as: "A state of uneasiness, apprehension, uncertainty, and fear resulting from anticipation of a realistic or fantasized threatening event or situation, often impairing physical and psychological functioning."

In other words, anxiety occurs when we behave (think and act) in an apprehensive manner, such as worrying about an event or situation. Anxiety is not a force or "thing" in itself. It's a state of uneasiness that arises, during the sales process, when we worry about what's to come, the unknown, what to say, or when to say it. Anxiety can produce many side effects, including:

- Numbness and tingling
- Dizziness
- Chest pain
- Headaches
- Neck tension
- Upset/nervous stomach
- Pulsing in the ear

- Burning skin
- Fear of impending doom
- Nausea
- Shortness of breath
- Electric shock feeling
- Shooting pains in the face
- Heart palpitations
- Weakness in legs
- Feeling like you are going crazy
- Inability to rest
- Sleep problems

Linda Wells, a world-renowned men's anxiety expert in New Zealand, says that sleeping problems are one of the biggest challenges and the first signs to watch for.

THE TRUTH ABOUT REJECTION

Even though we feel the pain of rejection and take it personally, I think it's important that we address the realities of rejection and what it really means.

People don't want to reject us. In fact, it pains them to turn you away and say no. Some people agonize over responding unfavorably in fear of losing your friendship. In reality, there is always going to be someone who rejects you because people prefer different things.

At times, I've tried to connect with potential clients who won't even return my calls or I contact them to arrange for a get-together but receive a lukewarm response.

Needless to say, rejection can be a real downer, especially when you're hoping for a positive outcome. No one likes to receive a "No," when it's so much better to get a "Yes." However, the only way to avoid rejections is to box yourself in, never leave your home, and avoid interacting with other people.

In reality, rejection is part of building your relationship muscle. I've learned that it's almost impossible to avoid rejection completely if you truly want to develop in sales and as a person. Rejection helps you to unearth the real you. Remember, you've got 999 opportunities just like Colonel Sanders, who was rejected 999 times.

So don't let rejection get you down. Remember, there is really nothing real about rejection. It's all about how we perceive the feeling. Rather than focus on the rejection, focus on the next prospect. Each time you are rejected, you have an opportunity to stay focused and move forward while trying once again to get it right.

Next!

"The aim of marketing is to know and understand the customer so well the product or service fits him and sells itself."

— Peter Drucker

CHAPTER 12

Networking for Success

Have you ever experienced running from one networking group to another, and then when you filed your taxes, it suddenly became clear that you had not made enough money to pay for all the fees, lunches, dinners, and breakfasts? That has happened to me too, and it didn't make me very happy.

AVOIDING BURNOUT

I've noticed lately that many entrepreneurs and coaches are beginning to get sick and drop out of sight to heal, rest, and recover. I totally get it! These people spend so much time running from one networking group, stage, or flight to the next that they become exhausted, overly stressed, and totally burnt out. You can tell it's coming when they start repeatedly saying they're tired, and then boom, some kind of illness pops up that takes them down for weeks and sometimes months.

To be honest, at one point I felt pretty tired and defeated, too, so I decided there had to be a way to do a better job of networking. And I found out I wasn't alone. Over a period of five years, I spoke to hundreds of entrepreneurs about what they thought was the answer to my networking failure. Strangely, the majority of them felt the same way I did. As a result, I learned some great ideas to share and I developed my own proven ideas. That is how the Five Networking Myths were birthed.

THE FIVE NETWORKING MYTHS

Myth 1: The more networking groups I attend the more money I'll make. It's the only way I can find someone to buy.

Truth: First of all, it's not about how many groups you attend. It's about the quality of those groups, the size, and the biggest question of all: Are they in your target market? Seeing networking members weekly may be comfortable and friendly, but it can also fool us into thinking we are really making an impact and the money is soon to come.

Myth 2: Breaking bread with other entrepreneurs is the most effective way to network.

Truth: Most of the networking groups have a cost. If you're paying for breakfast, lunch, and dinner like I was, you can't help but go in the hole unless you are able to sell your products or services to the attending members. We don't realize how much the costs of these communities add up until the end of the year when we're forced to file our taxes and face reality.

Remember, the numbers don't lie. If your numbers aren't adding up, it's time to rethink the amount of time and money spent on networking groups. Don't forget that driving to these events has a cost in time, gas, and wear and tear on your car, so consider them to be additional expenses along with the costs of membership and meals.

Myth 3: Staying with the same groups allows people to know, like,

and trust me.

Truth: We don't think to evaluate each networking group after six months. Ask yourself, "How much money did I make in the last six months from this group's members? How much did I make indirectly through referrals from these members? (If the answer is none, you better run.) But before running, ask yourself: Am I using the right message and the right words? Is this the right target market, and why aren't they hearing me?"

Weigh each group independently for profitability while weighing your income against the expenses of attendance. What are the results? Are you losing the money game, or are you a winner? If you're a loser, find another group and move on or start pouring on the Secret Sauce and change the way you define your business so your target market can understand your message.

Myth 4: There's plenty of money to go around and plenty of clients to serve.

Truth: We're all circulating the same money among small communities, and we can't afford to pay everyone we meet in these groups. To limit costs, many entrepreneurs trade or discount their products and services. Yes, we gain a great deal of knowledge and benefit from trades, but in exchange, we may have a challenge paying our bills, feeding our family, and feeling valued.

I'm not saying don't trade. Sometimes it's the smartest thing to do if you need something for your business and you don't have the money to pay for it. Think before you trade, and get an agreement in writing so no one feels cheated. If you do decide to trade, ask for a video testimonial from your satisfied customer.

Myth 5: We don't need to play a bigger game. All we need to do is raise our prices.

Truth: We are playing way too small and way too safe in our little networking groups. It's better to get more exposure to a broader range of people, who can afford your product or service, to make a bigger impact and more income.

If your programs and pricing are set to go, it's time to go bigger. Dare I say that some entrepreneurs even move to a new area to meet and mix with new people and find new clients? Yes, move. I did it myself, and it made a world of difference in my income.

RECOMMENDATIONS FOR NETWORKING SURVIVAL

Attend only one to three well-defined networking groups per month. The way to take back your money and time is to pick up the phone and interview the group's host. What do I mean by well-defined? Three quarters of the attendees must be in your target market. The host knows the answers to the following questions. If the answers aren't satisfactory to you, look for a different group.

1. **How many members belong to your group?** Look for groups of thirty-five members or more. Recently, I visited a group that was new and had only twelve members. I went twice and decided that the group was too small and only four of the twelve fit into my target market, so I decided to move on. I did, however, walk away with two new students in those two visits. As you are looking for a networking home, keep in mind that you can attend twice before paying for a membership. So visit lots of groups before deciding to join.

2. **What would you say is the age range?** A minimum of 75 percent of the members should fit into your target market. This will assist you greatly in making money. Remember, your tar-

get market focus is the key to your networking success.

3. **What is the average price point for what the members are willing to pay for a program or event?** I ask this because it provides a level of understanding for what the participants in the networking group can afford to pay for your product or programs. It also will give you an idea of whether you'll need to finance new clients or whether they can pay for the whole course all at once.

4. **Is there available parking around your event?** Going to downtown events with little or no parking will make your experience expensive, frustrating, and time-consuming. In San Diego, we are required to pay $20 for two hours at a downtown event.

5. **Will I have a speaking opportunity, and can I make an offer?** This is important if you want to speak about and give valuable tips regarding your work. You also might want to ask whether there is a fee to speak or a percentage of what you make that is a required payment to the event planner.

6. **What is the cost of a vendor table, and what's required to set one up?** It's important to weigh your costs versus the potential income. I once attended an event and purchased a $250 vendor table. I knew before I paid that I only needed one client to offset the cost of my presence at the event.

You've already determined who your target market is. Don't give in to joining a group simply because your friends are there. In fact, it's better if your friends aren't there. There's no point in networking with your friends. This is your business, not a social gathering. Let go of any or all networking groups that haven't contributed to your income unless you believe you didn't earn the income because you didn't know how to sell and weren't prepared.

You already know the people in my well-defined demographic are high-level entrepreneurs, coaches, and educators who want to provide their audiences with maximum benefit and income.

You wouldn't find me in a networking group with members who can only afford a maximum $297 purchase price point without keeping in mind that I'll need to offer a financing plan for any entrepreneurs who choose to take my programs. If money is tight for you and you can't afford to take payments, you may want to take this into consideration.

Entrepreneurs in the hobby zone are attending networking groups in hopes of connecting to make money. They aren't clear about who their perfect client is so they find themselves reaching out to everyone in the group. If you haven't done your homework and determined who your target market is, it's impossible to decide on the best use of your time. Do your homework so you can get out of the hobby zone and make the best use of your time and money.

It's not fair to attend or join a networking group without doing your research. It won't support you or the group if you haven't yet clarified whether the group fits into your plan. I also suggest that you do not take on a job in the networking group if there's no benefit to you. Recently, it was decided by an event planner that I would be the membership ambassador for a large group of ninety people who gather monthly here in San Diego. I wasn't asked, but I went along with it to see whether it would benefit my business. I held that position for six months and then decided to resign because there were no benefits. This is something you must do too. Evaluate every group you join very carefully and make decisions that benefit you and your income. I've done a lot of business in this group, and I've found that it's better to be networking among the members than to be a membership chair who is required to stand at the registration table.

Reviewing Your Current Networking Groups

Review the networking groups you are currently attending and re-move any from the list that haven't created an income for you in the past six months.

Next, choose three networking groups that zero in on your perfect clients. If you can't find groups that fit your target market, ask around for suggestions, join a group online that meets on Zoom, or create your own group on Meetup that is designed to call in your specific target market.

Be aware that your group will start small and build over time. How-ever, if you're good at your 3 Step Sales Waltz™, you only need one person to attend per week.

Limiting your networking attendance to your target market and at-tending only two or three groups per month, with high numbers of attendees, will save you money, time, and frustration, which will prevent burnout.

For years, I've been a part of the financial industry and have attend-ed meeting after meeting. One company had so many mandatory meetings that I wasn't able to find the time to be with and market to potential clients who would be interested in buying my service and products. Over and over again, I was expected to sit and listen to the same information, wasting valuable sales time. When I mentioned this to my superiors, they replied that I was required to sit with my people and not allowed to miss meetings. I didn't stay with the com-pany long after that because it was hurting my income.

I see this with a lot of MLMs (multi-leveling marketing organiza-tions). Two or three times a week, their salespeople are expected to attend meetings during valuable client time. In reality, this makes no sense because you can't sell to each other in the company. Once you've had enough training, you must get out of the comfort zone of the group to present your product or service in your networking groups.

FINAL THOUGHTS

1. Never ever remain in a group that doesn't fit into your target market.

2. Talk to the meeting organizer before attending the networking group.

3. Attend as many groups as you want twice, but know then you'll have to pay.

4. Stop hanging out with people selling in your same profession. They are your competitors, so why waste valuable sales time with people who already own and sell your products?

5. Hang out with friends at times other than during your work hours.

6. Review each group every six months, and if you've networked properly and didn't receive any business, leave the group and move on.

7. Avoid taking on positions in groups that offer no benefits

8. Choose only three networking groups per month to attend.

9. Play a bigger game and get online instead of driving in the traffic.

10. Get out of your comfort zone and start practicing the 3 Step Sales Waltz™.

The next step on our journey together is to learn how to overcome objections. This is one of my students' biggest challenges. They have so much fear that triggers around this question that they don't even want to talk to anyone about what they do or how they can support that person. "What if I don't know what to say?" they ask me, and you may be asking this too. That's why we'll address it next, and I know you'll be pleasantly surprised by how easy it is to overcome this fear.

"If you believe you are right, then you should believe that you can make the case that you're right. This requires you to deal with serious objections properly."

— Julian Baggini

♡

CHAPTER 13

Overcoming Objections Effectively

Most of my students tell me they're afraid to open a sales conversation because they either don't know how or they get tangled up in their words when a potential client raises an objection or asks a question they aren't prepared to answer. This seems to be one of the biggest fears to address.

In many companies, sales managers do their very best to increase sales, but they haven't been trained to provide high performance sales coaching. Companies do everything they know how to achieve their sales goals, and sales reps definitely want to achieve their sales quotas, but sales coaching is the only strategy that provides a high potential for bringing these two aspirations together.

Sales coaching is not a natural skill; it's a learned skill that brings about a great deal of effective change. Managers would be much more effective if they spent time in the field with their salespeople. US companies invest approximately $5 billion annually in sales training, but they tend to focus on sales methodology and sales training. Sales coaching is usually further down on the list.

A Sales Executive Council study showed that a 5 percent performance improvement from the "middle 60 percent" yields 70 percent more revenue than 5 percent improvement from the top 20 percent. Revenues would greatly improve if sales coaching was moved to the top and salespeople focused on dropping sales-y phrases and instead started relating to their clients in a way that builds authentic relationships.

This is a skill I teach in my Compel Don't Sell course. Active listening is one of the first steps to overcoming objections. In fact, if you listen very carefully and respond to your clients in their own words, they'll have no need to object.

Begin by finding out what your new friend wants and needs simply by asking the right questions that lead to connection and provide you important feedback. This simple technique makes it easy to determine how you can support your clients and quickly determine who does or doesn't need your support.

According to The Business Dictionary, the word "objection" means a formal protest or disapproval of something that has been said. You notice that it says "disapproval of something that has been said." It doesn't say that the disapproval is meant toward you personally or whatever it is you are selling. It is simply a disapproval of something that was said.

Keeping this fact in mind, we can move to the three standard objections: 1) not enough time, 2) not enough money, and 3) not enough clarity.

Not Enough Time: Almost everyone in Earth School has a very busy lifestyle. People tend to be stressed just meeting day-to-day demands, tending the children, making the almighty buck to put food on the table, and keeping up with appearances.

In the business world, entrepreneurs hire many coaches at a time who make a lot of demands on their time, so they'll often say, "I don't have enough time to take on another program. Let me get done with this one, and then we can talk again."

In this case, it's important to honor their space and schedule a follow-up call. If someone tells me, "I can't do this right now," I'll ask, "Is it no for now or no forever?" If the person says it's no for now, we make another appointment. If it's no forever, I thank the person for his honesty and am grateful that he didn't waste my time.

Not Enough Money: If a person says she doesn't have enough money, she may be telling you the truth, or she may not have enough clarity about what you are selling, or she may simply not want to spend the money.

Recently, I had a client decide to take my Business Mastery course. She was struggling financially, so we structured a program of payments that would be suitable for her monthly budget. She signed the agreement, and then we spent a great deal of time scheduling her coaching dates and setting her up to receive her modules. She received the benefit of two hours of coaching where we laid out her blueprint and goals.

Two weeks later, it became apparent that she was having extreme financial difficulties and couldn't meet the quotas with the company where she was working. I could feel her fear. I quickly told her that I understood her dilemma, so I would dissolve her contract. I believe it's extremely important that my community members continue to be supportive with each other because someone who is unhappy is like a cancer that festers over time and destroys heartfelt community relationships.

It was easy to see that my client thought there might be a battle, so she was audibly relieved when I released her so quickly. She said she was grateful and thanked me for my understanding. She made it clear she wanted to stay connected. During this conversation, I had the option of peace or pain. Which did I choose? Always think about your clients first before speaking so they know you care about them and their concerns.

I've witnessed as coaches, speaking from the stage, ratchet up event attendees to the point where attendees are running to the back of the room to spend their last dollars, max out their credit cards, wipe out their 401ks, or watch the last dollars in their bank accounts dissolve.

This is an impulse-buy that often won't last, providing the coach will release them from their contracts or they write letters dissolving the contracts within three days. On the other hand, I've seen entrepreneurs wind up living in their cars because they overspent on a program and received no results.

Even if 100 people don't run to the back of the room when you're on stage, if you get five to ten people who sign up for your program with integrity and the ability to pay, you will always have a pristine reputation connected to your brand. Integrity is everything. Remember, people are watching and talking. It's been said that each person knows at least seven people he can complain to, so if you choose to hurt one, you've hurt eight.

Not Enough Clarity: In some cases, the individual simply needs more clarity about your product, but she doesn't know the right questions to ask. Help her out. Ask, "What's coming up for you?" and she'll share her concern. This gives you an opportunity to respond by using a technique I'll teach you in Step 3 of the Sales Waltz in Chapter 17.

As a final thought, I want to reiterate that objections are not di-

rected at you, and the more questions a person asks, the more interested he is in what you are offering. If he's asking questions, he's
interested. High Cs need a lot of data and time to research, so give
them as much information and data as you possibly can. High Ds
are bottom line and will only want the definitive benefits. Evaluate
your clients after your first meeting so you can determine how best
to serve them during your next appointment.

"To succeed in life, you need three things: a wishbone, a backbone and a funny bone."

— Reba McEntire

♡

CHAPTER 14

Overcoming the Fear of Asking for Money

Holistic coaches have the biggest challenge with money and overcoming objections. They'd rather give their services away than have to go through the pain of asking for money. They are so deep into heart-centered giving that they often provide free services for people who *can* afford to pay.

These coaches deserve so much more than the little value they receive in return for their knowledge and services. Giving away the store causes one to feel the pain of not being appreciated, and in reality, they're not cherishing themselves because they receive little if any money to pay their bills or do the things they enjoy.

Have you ever felt this way? Health and wellness coaches are frequently afraid of feeling pushy, and they experience anxiety when asking for money. Sometimes they feel like they were given the gift of healing so they shouldn't ask to be paid for their work. This is simply not true. You were put here on earth to share and provide others with your gifts, but it's also important to thrive and enjoy your life. You were given this talent to share with others, and it's not expected that you do it for free.

In fact, your clients will often become very uncomfortable if you don't charge enough for your programs and services. It isn't fair to them to make them feel uncomfortable because you undervalue yourself; they may not work with you again because of that discomfort. Not charging enough or not charging at all creates a blind difficulty that neither you nor your client is comfortable bringing up because it's difficult to heal a discrepancy in how you see and value yourself.

Another challenge is that some people think money is dirty, so they fear that once they have it, they'll do despicable things to hurt others. This belief is reinforced by the way US politicians raise money from their constituents and then spend millions of dollars destroying their opponents' reputations. This may be the way politicians do things, but would you do that? I highly doubt it.

On the other hand, I did a bit of research on this "money is dirty" statement and found that the Dirty Money Project, in New York, has been studying our money for years and they've found that, "Each dollar bill carries roughly 3,000 types of bacteria on its surface." So, yes, it's been proven that money is dirty, but it's not dirty to have money, especially if you make and save enough to give to charity.

ASKING FOR MONEY

Asking people for money is probably the most difficult and the most important measure of how your business is performing. After all, how do we get you out of the hobby zone if you can't get beyond the fear of asking for the money that plays such a large part in how you live your lifestyle? Do you want to live under a bridge and eat out of a dumpster, or take a cruise and enjoy your favorite foods? It's your choice, and now is a good time to get beyond this faulty thought-process.

Asking a person for money face-to-face isn't always easy; it takes time to get comfortable with this skill. Not many entrepreneurs love to do it initially. In fact, most find this to be one of their biggest fears. Know that if you are afraid to ask for money, you're perfectly normal. If you are not afraid to ask for money, you get a high-five. You can stop reading and go ask somebody right now if he's ready to buy your program, and don't forget to get his credit card number.

A wide variety of reasons exist for why entrepreneurs are afraid to ask for money, so I'll address a few of them here. Let's take a look at the message sent in our American society. Even today, we're taught that there are four subjects we should never talk about in business, on a date, or in an effort to keep the peace around family. Those taboo topics are: politics, money, religion, and sex. We're also taught that "Those who have money received it by cheating others," "You must work hard for your money," and my personal favorite "There is never enough to go around."

Many of us were raised to believe that asking people what their salaries are or how much they paid for their houses or cars is rude. As a CFE Certified Financial Educator®, I frequently ask these questions and am comfortable in this role, but some will say, "I'm not used to being so upfront about my personal finances." And that's understandable since that's bred into us at an early age.

In my family, my father took care of all of the financial decisions. Sometimes, a wife doesn't even know how much money her husband earns, or how he spends the money, until he dies, and then she's shocked and overwhelmed to discover how in the dark she was. I never knew how much my father made when he was in business. Did you?

It's amazing how many people know nothing about the stock market, what the difference is between a "bear" and "bull" market, or what the rising or falling of the Dow Jones means for the economy, their 401ks, and their futures.

As a result of this secrecy, money tends to take on the relatively mysterious reputation of being bad. The hidden message is that good people don't deal with money except for survival.

Many people misquote the Bible, by saying, "Money is the root of all evil." Actually, the correct verse in the New Testament is, "For the love of money is the root of all evil: which while some coveted after, they have erred from the faith, and pierced themselves through with many sorrows" (1 Timothy 6:10, King James Version).

The only meaning money has is the meaning we create for it in our own minds. The word money is just that. It's a word. Its meaning is connected to what we've been taught as a core belief at a young age.

Money, simply put, facilitates our ability to buy what we want or need. There is nothing evil or shameful about it. Looking into your core beliefs around money will enable you to overcome these ill-conceived notions. You may find it interesting to learn how and why you were taught not to speak of money. Once you dig in and discover the thought process, you'll be able to overcome and reframe your meaning for money.

In reality, money has no intrinsic value. It is just a number on a piece of paper or a computer screen. The challenge is that we have all bought into the idea of assigning it value and meaning in our minds.

In the space below, write down your core beliefs around money, where the beliefs came from, and what you say to yourself around asking for money.

_____

_____

_____

_____

_____

_____

_____

_____

RETRAINING YOUR MIND

Unfortunately, most of us let our dreams and goals pass us by because of what we tell ourselves, and what we tell ourselves is usually not based in reality. Since the 1970s, I've questioned authority, the media, politicians, our educators, religion, and all varieties of rules that take away freedom of success and peace in my life.

Fears, created by authority, slow us down and keep us comfortably in a state of complacency. We believe we'll always be taken care of by our government, and the media instills fear into the masses to keep us controlled and focused on following the laws. The reality is that there isn't enough law enforcement to protect us, unless blood is drawn, and fewer and fewer people are applying to become members of law enforcement because so many are killed in the line of duty.

The power of the government, aligned with the media, is all an illusion. This is evidenced by how we are all meant to be on guard and watching everyone around us since the September 11, 2001 terrorist attacks. Now we're supposed to be afraid of each other, and this shows up considerably at the airports where we're governed by our primary colors. "Be alert," the sound system says. "We are now on yellow alert." Be cautious, and if you see anything suspicious, report it immediately. Fear, fear, and more fear. This is why we stay in our comfort zone, focusing on just getting by without getting into trouble, but even that doesn't work.

In my courses, I talk about the fact that when we arrive here on earth, we know nothing. We are clean and pure little beings full of love and acceptance. As we grow, our parents teach us what foods we're supposed to like, how to dress, and what not to do that could lead to a timeout if we disobey. We're told, "Don't touch that or you'll get hurt," "Don't talk like that or you'll lose this," and "Knock it off or I'll text your dad."

Raising children today is all about threats, consequences, and instilling fear into young minds. This limits freedom of thought, creativity, and individualism, and it is the beginning of controlled conformity and the dissolution of individualism, trusting relationships, and developing love among our brothers.

As children, we haven't learned how to discern what is right for us because discernment comes with experience. Discernment is developed over time. Neuroscientists, marketers, advertisers, media, religions, and governments are well-aware of the power of training your mind at a young age by instilling ideas they want us to believe are true.

When I was young, we thought smoking and drinking were cool because we saw people in commercials smoking and drinking. It was okay for women to be treated despicably and for men to drink on the job because it was displayed in the media and people tend to believe that what we see in the media provides credibility. That's why I tell you that it's important to become visible to your target market on media and the web.

The experts know our minds are greatly affected when triggered by sight or sound. The best example I have for this is how sight and sound affected me at a very young age and left a lasting impression. *The Three Stooges* used to be a program my brother, who is two years younger, and I watched weekly. We hung on every word and thought much of it was funny. If you've seen this program, you know that the

Three Stooges hit each other, act stupid, and make ridiculous noises for no apparent reason. It was, however, very entertaining for both of us. After about two months, my brother, who was eight at the time, began to mimic their actions. He began hitting kids at school and making stupid noises in class. Obviously, the Three Stooges had quite an effect on my brother, and it wasn't long before the program was designated by my mom as off limits. Advertisers are well-aware of the effects TV has on children, which is why they spend so much money advertising toys and kids' foods during the cartoons they watch. According to the Campaign for a Commercial Free Childhood (www.commercialfreechildhood.org):

- Companies spend about $17 billion annually marketing to children, a staggering increase from the $100 million spent in 1983.

- Children under 14 spend about $40 billion annually. Compare this to the $6.1 billion that 4-12 year olds spent in 1989. Teens spend about $159 billion.

- Children under 12 influence $500 billion in purchases per year.

- This generation of children is the most brand-conscious ever. Teens between 13 and 17 have 145 conversations about brands per week, about twice as many as adults. The website goes on to say children ages 2-11 see more than 25,000 advertisements a year on TV alone, a figure that does not include product placement. Children are also targeted with advertising on the Internet, cell phones, mp3 players, video games, school buses, and in school.

- Almost every major media program for children has a line of licensed merchandise, including food, toys, clothing, and accessories. Brand-licensed toys accounted for $22.3 billion in 2006.

- In their effort to establish cradle-to-grave brand loyalty and promote nagging, marketers even target babies through licensed toys and accessories featuring media characters.

- Viral marketing techniques take advantage of children's friendships by encouraging them to promote products to their peers.

In another example, imagine a seven-year-old child who is challenged at school. He is repeatedly rewarded with a happy face if he's good and punished with a sad face if he is challenged that day. Our children read our faces for love and acceptance, so being controlled by a stamped red sad face on a simple piece of white paper, and verbally told why he received the sad face is devastating for him and creates a vicious circle of anxiety.

This child feels as if he isn't being seen, that no one likes him, that what he wants isn't heard, and he's confused about why. He demands, whines, cries, and bullies to get attention, even if it's negative, and as a result, the discipline directed at him continues to grow stricter. His toys are taken away and he receives more sad faces. It's painful to watch and painful for him because he is a round creative peg who is daily being forced to conform toward becoming crammed into a square hole.

Worse yet, there is absolutely no meaning in the color red, the sad face, or the paper with this symbolism attached to it. It is all given meaning through the creation of pain. In and of themselves, the symbols mean nothing except to train a seven-year-old mind to believe in the administration and conform into one teacher's way of thinking and discipline. It's a shame, but over time, out of pain, he may conform into whoever others perceive him to be because they will convince him too that he is bad.

When we tell ourselves something disempowering, we lose our freedom to discern and take action for our wellbeing. Whatever you tell yourself in this moment, you instantly become. In the example of this beautiful child, the sad face tells him he is bad and, therefore, he thinks he is bad and continues to bully others and act badly thereby, reinforcing that he is bad with more red sad faces. It's a vicious circle. All this child wants is to be seen, understood, and loved, which would bring out his creativity and allow him to flourish and shine.

It's imperative that we listen carefully to what we say to ourselves and don't take unkind comments from others too seriously. Yes, if they suggest a change in behavior in earnest with love in their hearts, then take it to heart and consider it carefully. But not everyone is well-meaning, and many times they want a change in you to satisfy their own agendas.

Personally, I use "I AM" affirmations. The all-powerful "I AM" presence is considered to be the first expression in individualization. According to Saint Germain and Guy Ballard's *The "I AM" Discourses, Volume III*: "The first expression of every individual, everywhere in the Universe either in spoken word, silent thought or feeling, is 'I AM' recognizing Its Own Conquering Divinity."

We identify ourselves as "I," "My," or "I am." "I am hungry," "I am sick," "I am tired," "I am broke." All of these statements identify you as the person in the action. When you say, "I cannot," "I have not," you are setting into motion limitless energy and a vibratory action that goes to work creating exactly what you say or think. We send thoughts out into the universe ignorantly and without thinking that bind us into either negative or positive results. It's entirely up to you because you are using, "the Most Divine Principle of Activity in the Universe: "I AM." When you say, "I AM sick," you are literally reversing the Principle of Life, which according to *The "I AM" Discourses* is naturally all perfection.

Stop! Think about what you are saying. Stop giving power to others, outer conditions, places, and things that cause you to live a painful life. Remember, you're striving for peace in your life and success in your business. Saying, "I can't sell," "I hate sales," "Everyone rejects me," or "I can't ask for money" creates exactly that. You won't be able to sell because every time you try to sell, something will happen that makes you hate sales; everyone will reject you every time you attempt to makes a sale, and you'll never make money because you believe and say you can't ask for money.

Instead, say, "I am abundantly wealthy and money is showered on me every day. In fact, I make so much money that I feel confident enough to give money away to charity. I am grateful for all of the goodness I have in my life, and I know there is so much more to come."

Even if you aren't feeling like you're in a positive place, keep in mind that you may have been wallowing in the negative, and it takes the strength of a new belief and speaking out loud a new perspective of what you want and desire in order to turn your life around. Try it right now. Write down three new beliefs and five things you are grateful for. You'll be amazed what a difference it makes to be genuinely grateful for all you do have when you stop whining about what you don't have.

My New Positive Beliefs:

1. _____

2. _____

3. _____

4. _____

5. _____

6. _____

"I AM" Grateful For:

1. _____

2. _____

3. _____

4. _____

5. _____

UNDERSTANDING BELIEF SYSTEMS

Only two types of beliefs really exist: fixed universal beliefs and flexible beliefs. Let's explore each one.

Fixed Universal Beliefs: The vast majority of humanity generally agrees upon these beliefs. We have universal laws as a result of fixed beliefs. The Law of Gravity or the fact that humans cannot breathe underwater are examples of universal laws that have been proven scientifically.

To accomplish breaking through the belief of a fixed universal law requires a clear understanding of the universal law, creative energy, and innovative thinking. An example of this is the flight of airplanes breaking through the law of gravity and scuba gear that allows for discovery and breathing on the ocean floor.

Flexible Beliefs: A flexible belief is one that doesn't need a solution. It simply needs a shift in perception, action, attention, practice, and knowledge. A flexible belief is subject to change and isn't considered to be either right or wrong. It depends on the individual's point of view. An example is the meaning of the red sad faces, the yellow warning color at the airport, or the thought that money is dirty. Beliefs, such as these, can be molded any way you choose with a simple shift in perception, a watchful eye, and a change in the practice of what you tell yourself.

Questioning our belief systems is the mechanism for shifting our consciousness as well as that of humanity. Over time, these shifts produce much greater and deeper levels of freedom by eliminating fear and anxiety.

SHIFTING OLD BELIEFS

In order to shift personal core beliefs and negative points of view to create solutions and success in your business, you must first decide whether your core belief is fixed or flexible, and then you must invent or discover a practice that sharpens your skills and creates new and better outcomes.

In the case of money being dirty, you can decide that money is only energy, and if you have your arms and hands stretched out to send and receive this energy, the thought of money will no longer be dirty. If, however, you hold your hands tightly against your chest, you will restrict the energy and create lack in your life. All that is required is simply to create a shift in the energy you perceive money to be.

Ask yourself, "What am I telling myself about this belief?" Then evaluate problems and challenges as they come up for you. When you say to yourself, "I'm broke," think about why you are saying that, where it comes from, and realize that every time you say that, you will most certainly remain broke. Whatever you believe is exactly what you receive.

Belief systems of any kind put your awareness to sleep. Losing awareness will create a loss of everything else, and you will be easily manipulated because you aren't focused and paying attention. Are you living in habitual patterns and accepting the status quo? Challenging your flexible beliefs will provide for more income, success in your business, and a much better lifestyle. Are your flexible beliefs impairing or empowering your potential?

Unhealthy support systems can make us feel incapable of making our own decisions. When we're looking outside of ourselves for love and approval, we become susceptible to manipulation and someone else's agenda just like a small child. This causes us to lose our critical-thinking skills and discernment.

Learning and taking action on new information that runs counter to current belief systems isn't easy. I see a great deal of this confusion when I suggest to my clients that they stop paying into their 401ks and explain that their employer's contributions in all probability won't overcome the volatility losses in the market.

Since this concept is foreign to them and goes against conventional societal thinking, they can't quickly wrap their minds around it. When I go on to say there are things they can do with their hard-earned income that will never lose money and probably double it, their first thought is always, "What about the taxes?"

Here lies the true essence of conditioning—the fear of paying taxes.

Just the thought of paying more taxes creates a conflicting idea in their minds. This thought process suggests that our core belief and inner drive are to do what's comfortable rather than buck the system and the beliefs it's instilled in us, even if doing so will benefit us.

Before 2007–2008, I read the same white paper report that Bill Clinton read, and based on reviewing the mortgage applications that were processed across the nation, it was obvious what was coming. At that time, I owned a nationwide business with 23,000 trained notary-signing agents who were processing mortgage documents as fast as people could put pen to paper.

Armed with this information, I told everyone who would listen to get out of the market as soon as possible. Some did but most didn't because the market was soaring at the time. "Oh, you're just doom and gloom. I'm not going to do that," said one of my dearest friends. Three months later, at the age of sixty-seven, she lost two million dollars. "I can't believe it, Shirlene. I just lost two million dollars in the market. What am I going to do? I've lost it all," she told me. All I could reply was, "Hmm, I'm sorry to hear that." Of all the people who should have listened to my advice, it should have been her. But why didn't she listen? She simply couldn't be flexible enough in her beliefs to protect herself. I should have sent her a red sad face in the mail with the words, "Bad girl for not listening to such an important warning."

Taking in new information and challenging belief systems is not easy. However, not doing so can cause discomfort and raise a great deal of fear very quickly. We obviously have strong inner drives to hold onto what we believe in an effort to prove to ourselves that we are right. We avoid the discomfort of making a change, even if presented with factual information because it may conflict with our existing ideas, beliefs, or values.

Instead, we complacently follow along behind the media and others who lead with authority. Why do so many believe mainstream media without consideration for what it's telling us? Millions of people, across the nation, are waking up to the influential flaws provided by mainstream media and disconnecting network TV. We need to learn to think for ourselves, question our beliefs, and open our minds to the idea of stepping outside of customary beliefs if we want to better our lives and create successful businesses.

In an article in *The Huffington Post*, Rabbi Shmuly Yanklowitz wrote, "Critical thinking and argument skills—the abilities to both generate and critique arguments—are crucial elements in decision-making." Without the critical-thinking ability, we cannot discern what is best for ourselves and we give away our power.

Having the ability to think strategically and objectively, while weighing factual information, are vital tools to be used along with your intuitive gut feelings. Focus on critical thinking skills, and with passion, practice taking action-oriented, mindful thought processes into all of your decision-making practices.

LET'S REVIEW

1. Your services have value, so you must charge a competitive fee to provide comfort for your clients and feelings of value for yourself.

2. You were put here on earth to provide value and a service that provides a benefit for your clients.

3. Dirty money is only a perception created by those who spend it to hurt others. You would never do that.

4. Asking for money was only a fear because of the mystery that society creates around talking about money. Now that you are able to reframe the thought of money as energy that you can

circulate through your hands, it is easier to ask for what you deserve to be paid.

5. It's important to think for yourself and be open to weighing facts, along with gut feelings, before making important decisions about your life.

6. Making complacent decisions based on societal norms presented by the media damages your business, sales success, income, and lifestyle.

Now it's your turn to reflect on your thoughts and beliefs around money. How have they shifted?

_____

_____

_____

_____

_____

Do you feel more comfortable about asking for money for your products, programs, or services? Why?

_____

_____

_____

_____

_____

What are the four steps you are willing to take to empower your potential?

1. _____

   _____

2. _____

   _____

3. _____

   _____

4. _____

   _____

We will go deeper into money know-how in the last section of this book after we discover how to maximize your wealth through media and speaking.

"I like to think of sales as the ability to gracefully persuade, not manipulate, a person or persons into a win-win situation."

— Bo Bennett

CHAPTER 15

Initiating the Sales Conversation

STEP ONE OF THE 3 STEP SALES WALTZ™

Armed with confidence and an understanding of your value, it's time to step into the sales arena and learn how to easily open a conversation with a potential client. At this point, you are only looking to connect with those you've selected as your target market. Anyone you speak with who isn't a part of your group will become a referral partner.

This chapter is all about strengthening your active listening muscle, and I promise it will be lighthearted and much easier than you might think.

OPENING YOUR FIRST SALES CONVERSATIONS

Let's begin with identifying how to open a conversation. It's really very easy and goes something like this: "Hi, Paula. How are you doing?" "Great!" she answers. I bet you're thinking, *Well, I could have said that, but it's after that when it gets sticky. Where do we go from there?*

This first step in the 3 Step Sales Waltz™ works with every personality type, and I use it because everyone, at least everyone I've met, is more relaxed talking about him- or herself. If it's someone I don't know, I'll say, "It's so great to meet you. Tell me about *you*."

That one question is all it takes and the person is off and running. If it's someone I've met previously, I'll say, "So great to see you again, Paula. It's been a while. What's happening with you?" or "How are things with your business?" or "How's the family?" Ask anything that pertains to what you already know about the person. If you can't remember anything about the person, but she seems to remember you, simply say, "Hi, Paula. Great to see you. Tell me what's going on with you."

The idea is to get the other person talking while remembering that the one who is asking the questions is the one in control of the conversation. But you must do your part too. You need to be a good listener, and I can't stress that enough. The person may share some really juicy information that will support you in the sales process later.

You might also be able to refer this person to someone who can support her if she isn't a perfect client for you. In this case, you are a hero for two people. Okay, so you weren't able to make a sale, but you were able to help both the person you gave the referral to and the person you took the time to listen to. Don't you think both will remember you in the future with a referral? Of course, they will.

Even if the person asks you what you do, you must not talk about yourself or what you sell. You can breeze over it and say something like: "I work with business owners to (whatever you do)," and then ask a question about what the other person was talking about. Always steer the conversation back to the other person and deflect it away from you.

All you want to do is get to know who this person is. This conversation is not about what you want or what you're selling.

Everyone wants to feel heard and cared for. This is why the first step in the 3 Step Sales Waltz™ is simply a reconnection or a get-to-know-you meeting. The minute you jump the gun and begin talking about you, the game is over and you lost.

You must learn to hold back your agenda in favor of making a new friend. Once you've shown that you care, your new acquaintance will be more open to asking what you do. Sometimes she'll even say to you in the next conversation, "We talked all about me last time. Now I'd like to learn about you." Talk about music to your ears! However, if you haven't taken the time to listen in the first step, she'll never have an interest in learning about you.

SELLING MODE NO-NOs

People get really turned off by words and phrases that sound and make them feel like they're being sold. Real estate is painfully guilty in this area because the agents develop sales-y phrases. Here's an example of what I mean. If you ask an agent, "How's the market?" he'll respond with something like, "Well, that depends. Are you looking to buy, sell, rent, or invest?" when he could say something like, "Have you been looking at houses? We could go down the street and look together. Do you have a little time?" Real estate agents are so pre-scripted that they launch into old scripted verbiage without even thinking about it.

I love teaching at real estate and mortgage companies because it makes a huge difference in the agents' income and how they relate authentically to their clients. A way to shift out of the sales-y concept is to think about other human beings as individuals rather than as sales prospects who need to be pushed and hammered into completing a sale. Stop with the sales jargon. "Do you want to buy or do you want to sell?" is not a caring question that builds relationships.

Now, you may be thinking, *Shirlene, I'm not going to do what you're suggesting. That won't work for me and I won't get as high of a closing ratio.* And I say to you: "Me, me, me, me, me." It's all about you thinking about yourself and not caring for or focusing on your clients.

Building relationships creates a referral base of people who care about who you are as a sales agent. This is all part of networking. Go out, be social, listen to what others have to say, make friends, and build lots of relationships.

EXERCISING ACTIVE LISTENING

Active listening is a skill that develops over time. Believe me; we aren't born with it. It's all about being genuinely interested in what another person is saying. To do this, you must forget about everything but the person you are interacting with. If you get distracted, the person will see and feel it immediately, and then you've lost him. The rule is never ever to let the person you are listening to feel like you didn't care enough to listen to the answer he shared.

I heard someone say once, "We have two ears and one mouth, so we should be listening twice as much as we speak." If you're a talker, that behavior needs to be curbed. You'll be amazed by what you hear if you aren't doing all of the talking. What you learn from those around you can truly enhance your business, unless it's gossip.

If you are talking about others, you'll sink your own ship. I know of a woman who did this, and pretty soon, her comments were heard in so many networking groups that she had to move to another state, leave her business, and get a job. Don't get caught in this predicament, and don't be fooled into thinking you can tell just one person you can trust. It's better not to say anything at all and keep your comments to yourself.

While you're chatting with someone, look at him with interest and connect. Nod your head to make sure he knows you're listening and make an effort to ask questions for clarification. Focus on what he's saying to make him feel important and heard. After all, we all want that, don't we? This is what I mean when I say, "Learn how to sell through your heart."

Make a heart connection and the other person will feel it. He'll never forget that you cared enough to stop and listen without quickly running by on the way to your next appointment. Let him know that you care about his concerns, struggles, and aspirations.

When you ask questions, don't make it sound like you are interrogating the person. It needs to be lighthearted and caring. Practice with your spouse or a good friend. Simply call the other person in the evening and ask, "Hey, James. How was your day?" James will be blown away that you cared enough to ask, and believe me, he will tell you.

I had a student ask, "What do you do when the person you are talking to won't shut up?" The answer is to do *nothing* but politely listen. He is feeding you very important information, and if you're on the phone, take notes like crazy. He will give you great feedback on how he feels about what you are doing, and maybe he'll even tell you how you can do it better. That would be a big help, wouldn't it?

Remember, the game is only to remain quiet and listen. When the person says something that is a direct hit on a concern you can solve, your tendency may be to jump in and begin your sales pitch. Instead, restrain yourself. Do not leap in for the kill or you will lose.

Here's what you can say when the potential client has just made a comment that your expertise can solve or support. "I might have an idea that would support you in resolving that, but we can talk about it later." This will stick in the back of his mind, as a tease that keeps him wondering long after you've parted, *I wonder what she knows that would work to get me past this?* It will also prompt him to call you for a second appointment.

If you're standing with the person, move to a quiet place as soon as you've finished the conversation and write down a few notes on the back of a business card or type it into your phone. This information is golden. We discussed the importance of speaking your clients' perfect words, and how to get those words and phrases in Chapter 9. When overcoming objections, all you are required to do is listen to your client's needs and then feed your client's phrases back to him when he is feeling insecure about his decision or experiencing fear or frustration when making a decision.

As we get deeper into the sales process, I'll show you how to use these conversations to create sales. Understand that not every conversation is with someone who might be a client, but never forget that each person you speak with knows a minimum of seven people he or she could refer you to if you've taken the time to show you care.

TIME FOR PRACTICE

To succeed with this first step of the 3 Step Sales Waltz™, there are two things you need to do: 1) Build your active-listening muscle, and 2) Practice. Let's look at each of these in-depth.

1.   Build Your Active-Listening Muscle

Now it's time for you to practice building your active-listening muscle. You can do this exercise with anyone you feel comfortable with. The exercise's purpose is to catch yourself when you find your mind wandering to somewhere other than the person who is speaking.

When you catch yourself wandering off, bring your mind back as soon as you notice. This step will support you in building your awareness muscle. If this step isn't easy for you, choose more people to listen to. Do not move to the next step until you've gotten good at this step.

Most of us have so much on our minds that it's difficult to stay focused on one conversation at a time. That's why it's important to practice becoming an active listener. This one activity will benefit you greatly. It's a confidence builder, and it will support your efforts to listen with your heart and show you care. Try not to jump into the conversation with your thoughts or coaching ideas. Give the person an opportunity to say whatever she wishes. Ask questions to show your interest and I promise she'll feel heard. However, as soon as you jump in and take over the conversation, you'll see the frustration in her facial expression.

Choose three people to interact with and practice this step. At this point, it should be only people you are familiar with. Do not choose someone who doesn't talk much. If you do, he or she will be the one asking you questions, and you will lose control of the conversation.

After each conversation, write answers to the following questions. (You may want to keep a journal since you'll have multiple conversations).

Who did you choose for this exercise, and why did you choose that person?

What was it like to be an active listener?

_____

_____

_____

How did it feel to you, and where in your body did you feel it?

_____

_____

_____

Did you feel a rush of energy to talk, but succeed in holding back?

_____

_____

_____

Did you succumb to being a chatty Kathy, dominating the conversation with coaching ideas?

_____

_____

_____

Were you able to maintain control of the conversation with clarifying questions?

_____

_____

_____

If not, why not? What happened that threw you off?

_____

_____

_____

What will you do better next time?

_____

_____

_____

Remember, there are no mistakes, only golden lessons. You have three opportunities to exercise your confidence-building, active-listening muscle. Each opportunity will make you stronger. Practice. Practice. Practice.

2. Practice

Now it's time to practice opening sales conversations with people you've never met. You can practice this step at any networking group. There are always people we haven't met, so it's a great opportunity to practice your opening sales conversation. Just before you go to the event, re-read the information provided in this chapter. Make sure your memory is fresh and go in confident. Speak with three new people and then fill in the blanks below for each of the three people you experience.

Answer these questions:

Write each person's name here:

1. _____

2. _____

3. _____

What does each person do for work?

1. _____

2. _____

3. _____

What was each person's primary line of conversation?

1. _____

2. _____

3. _____

What were the expressed concerns on each person's mind?

1. _____

2. _____

3. _____

What are the benefits you can provide for each person?

1. _____

2. _____

3. _____

What is the biggest challenge around their business or lifestyle?

1. _____

2. _____

3. _____

Would you meet with this person again?

1. _____

2. _____

3. _____

How did it feel to open a conversation with a new person?

1. _____

2. _____

3. _____

How did it feel when you resisted the temptation to launch into what you do or use a sales-y phrase?

1. _____

2. _____

3. _____

One of the major challenges you'll find in Step 1 is that surge of energy that makes you want to jump in and coach. That's a big no, no. As soon as you feel that urge, stop talking. The trick is to recognize it when you begin to feel it. Don't worry; you will jump the gun and walk away kicking yourself more than once. We all do. You'll know because the person will lose interest almost immediately, and it's hard to recover the relationship when you make it all about you. Focus on remaining interested in the new friendship you're building. Practice, practice, practice.

Another catch will be when the person asks you what you do. *What then?* you must be wondering. Remember, it's not your turn. We'll talk more about this in Step 2 in the next chapter. You don't get to talk about yourself until Step 2. When they ask what you do, give a brief statement. I might say. "I work with entrepreneurs struggling with sales. Tell me more about you. How long have you been in business?" or I might say, "How are you doing with your business? Are you selling lots of programs?" Then they'll go on and talk more about themselves.

Once you've practiced Step 1, move on to the next chapter and learn about Step 2. In Step 2, you get to be the star and talk about you.

"Don't practice until you get it right.
Practice until you can't get it wrong."

— Mike Ferry, Real Estate Sales Trainer

♡

CHAPTER 16

Waltzing Through Step Two

In our sales process, the purpose of any appointment is only to establish a relationship, build trust, and set the next appointment. Notice that I didn't say the purpose is to sell your prospect on your product or service. If you dance through the 3 Step Sales Waltz™ properly, the process itself will make the sale. In other words, if you practice active listening, use the words your clients are waiting to hear, and restrain yourself from pouncing on the sales process, you will make the sale without the need for overcoming objections or rejection. Your clients will sell themselves if they trust and believe that what you told them will truly resolve their pain.

If you didn't have much time to talk with your potential client during the first meeting, the second meeting in this process will give you more information and perhaps time to share what you do to support your clients. This appointment can be done on the phone or in person over tea. Skype works great too if distance is a challenge. I love chatting with my clients on Skype while sipping on tea.

My conversations start with, "Hi, Julia. It's so great to connect with you again. How are you? Do tell." I say this in a sing-song voice with a big smile. After all, I am genuinely happy to see my new friend again, and it's important to begin with catching up since your first connection. At this point, I'll say, "I was thinking about you. There wasn't a lot of time to chat when we met last, and I wondered whether you'd share more about your progress regarding…" (whatever tidbit you learned regarding how you could support her in the last conversation). Again, you are controlling the conversation. Hopefully, you made an effort to write down the high points of your first conversation or it will be difficult to continue the conversation

It's been scientifically proven that women need to talk and hear themselves in the conversation, so if your potential client is a woman, it's important to give her the first opportunity to share and catch up. Once her need to talk has been expressed, she'll ask you a question and perhaps give you an opportunity to share what you do.

FOCUS ON THE MIDDLE WAY

This is your time to shine, but be aware of that rush of energy that occurs just before you begin to explain. Do not let it overtake you. Breathe before you start and remain calm. Explain your expertise in one to three sentences ending with, "And that's why I was thinking about you. I wondered whether you might like an idea for how to solve the challenge you're experiencing." Then stop and be silent. Even if it takes what seems like an eternity, wait. She must respond before you move forward with your idea. Her response gives you the green light to begin. If you don't get the green light, change the subject or let her guide you to the next topic.

Once you get the green light, begin by repeating her own words and phrases back to her. These are the words you heard during the first meeting. "I remember you said…blah blah blah, and I was thinking that I might be able to support you with an idea. Would you like to know more?" Again, wait for the green light response before explaining what your idea is. In each step, your client is giving you permission to move forward with a yes. When you get three yeses and a positive lean-in response, you've got a sale.

Let me give you an example of one of my own conversations....

Whether it's massive visibility for massive income or the certified financial educator side of my business, people always come to me with income challenges, angst over losing money in the market, and concerns over paying too much in taxes. For this example, I'll structure this conversation around money as the bottom line concern.

Many times at networking groups, someone I don't know, and have never met, will make a beeline across the room to connect with me. They often say, "Hi, I'm Julia. I see you everywhere, and I'm so excited to meet you finally." You and I both know that they don't see me everywhere, but they think they do because I post so many videos and blog posts that they think they know me personally. That's a good thing, right? It's validation that my marketing is working.

I respond with, "Hi, Julia. It's great to meet you. Tell me about you. I'm excited about getting to know you." Now she has the floor and I've got the control. Sweet! As I mentioned before, invariably the topic of money comes up because of something she saw in one of my many video tips.

During the first conversation, I learn that Julia is frustrated because she can't seem to get any sales and she was told that attending networking groups is the only way to get business. At this point, she is close to running out of money because she's paying for branding, marketing, and lots of networking meals. I set the next appointment by saying, "It's difficult to talk here. How about we schedule a time to chat, and perhaps I can offer some suggestions that might help." People normally agree and are surprised that I am willing to give them some of my time. In Julia's case, I write on the back of her card where I met her and what her needs are as a reminder for our future conversation.

After the event, I follow up with a quick little message about how nice it was to meet her and include my email scheduler to set the next appointment for a chat over tea on Skype. When the day arrives, I review my notes and focus on this one conversation with this one person. I'm ready for active listening. Everything else is cleared from my mind. I breathe deeply and manifest a positive conversation that truly supports my new friend and my business.

"Hey, there. How are you, Julia?" I say when she appears on Skype. "It's great to see you again. How have you been since we chatted last?" I know to let her talk until she's finished filling me in.

"You know, Julia, I was thinking about you and what you shared when we spoke last. If I remember correctly, you mentioned that you are challenged because you've been attending so many networking groups, building your brand, and spending money on your business, but there hasn't been much income. Did I get that right?"

At this point, Julia feels cared for and is impressed that I would actually remember what she shared. This begins to build trust. She can tell that I cared enough to listen to how she was feeling.

"Yes, you got that right," she says. "That's exactly what I'm experiencing."

And then I say, "So, tell me more about what's going on." Notice that I took control of the conversation from the very beginning.

Eventually, Julia will get around to saying, "I was wondering what you meant when you said you might have a suggestion for me." This is music to my ears. It's my lead in for the sales conversation.

"Well, I was wondering whether you might be open to some ideas about how to resolve and overcome your income challenges. I've tried this with other clients and it's worked very well."

"Absolutely, I'd be open. What would you suggest?"

"May I ask a couple of questions for clarification? I don't want to interfere with anyone else who might be coaching you." (This question will determine whether there is someone she is currently paying for guidance.)

"No, there's no one. I think that's why I'm confused. I can't figure out what to do next."

"What if I could show you a way to get over the hurdle and make more money? Would that be a good thing to know?"

"Yes, it would. In fact, it would make a big difference because if I don't figure out how to make an income, I'll have to go get a job."

"Getting a part-time job might be a good idea to tide you over until your business is providing a solid income that covers your expenses. In the meantime, we can work together to build a solid foundation for your business, and when you reach the same amount of income in your business that your job pays, you can quit. That's just an idea that you can think over."

"That's not a bad idea. What should I do about my business?"

"First, you want to determine your target market. Have you already decided whom that might be?"

"I want to help anyone who needs me."

"That's wonderful in theory, but it's quite a challenge because it's too broad. How will you know whom to market to? Did you know that different target markets are looking for different words?"

"What do you mean?"

"If you don't define your target market, and use the words people in that market are wanting to hear, they will get confused because they don't understand you. Would it be okay if I share a story about what one of my clients recently experienced and how we turned her business into a $30,000 machine?"

"Sure. I'd love to hear it."

"My client is an expert at coaching businesses on how to work with internal relationship challenges. She also works with solopreneurs to develop relationship-building skills. She was using the same speech for both audiences with no sales results from either market. So we worked together to define and refine a speech for each market, while speaking the words each client base wanted to hear. Now she's selling up a storm. She didn't realize that her two target markets speak different languages and that all she needed to do was change her language in each speech to make the sales. Does that make sense to you?"

"Wow, I never thought of that."

"I spoke with her just two days ago and she had made a $30,000 sale, and all we did was tweak the words she was using. Pretty cool, don't you think?"

"I want to do that. What a difference it would make in my bank account. How do you know what words to use?"

"You can do this just like she did. Actually you have two choices: You can attend my Compel Don't Sell two-day intensive course, or you can work with me one-on-one and get the same results she did. Why don't you think about it and we can meet again."

"Okay. When shall we meet?"

"Let's set it up right now. Let's take a look at our calendars. Does next week on Wednesday work for you?"

"Yes, how about 11 a.m.?" She's closing me for the appointment.

"Pacific time?"

"Yes. I'm looking forward to meeting with you again, and I appreciate the time you spent with me. I learned a lot."

"You got it, and I'm glad our time together was productive for you. I'll see you Wednesday at 11 Pacific time on Skype. Have a great week."

"You too. Thanks. Bye-bye."

Step 2 of the 3 Step Sales Waltz™ is now complete, and because I didn't rush in to sell my program, my potential client is given the space and time to think about how what I just shared will make a difference in her business. In fact, she'll be chomping at the bit by the following Wednesday, eager to get started on her road to income success.

Was I rejected by what I suggested to Julia? Will I need to struggle to overcome objections? No, absolutely not and this is why:

- We had a caring one-on-one conversational connection.

- I showed Julia that I cared enough to listen and remember the concerns she expressed in our first connection.

- I made an effort to provide one-on-one time, just for her.

- I gave her reasonable ideas for how she could overcome her challenges.

- I mentioned that I'd been thinking about her since we last met.

- I suggested that she go back to work part-time to relieve the stress and tension of not having enough money to cover her bills.

- Most importantly, I didn't rush to sell her my coaching program before she had time to think over the ideas I shared that would save her business.

Did Julia receive value from our forty-minute chat over tea? She certainly expressed that she did.

Now it's your turn to practice this technique, but only after you've made a conscious effort to complete the active listening exercise in the last chapter. You might want to find a partner to work with to support you. That way, you can refine conversations that will lead to an easy sales close, which is exactly what we do in the third step of the 3 Step Sales Waltz™.

I'm excited about your success in the sales process. After you've practiced the first two steps, you'll find them to have a natural, easy flow. I always keep a list of the names I'm working on and note 1, 2, or 3 for where we are in the 3 Step Sales Waltz™ process. Each step requires a week of breathing room before the next connection.

When you get good at this process, you'll be making millions and I'll be able to say, "I knew you when…."

If you feel and believe that my coaching is a good fit, I'm always here for you, or better yet, register for the next Compel Don't Sell two-day intensive course at ShirleneReeves.com. Once you've completed the two-day intensive, you'll be invited to attend my ninty-day weekly Sales Boot Camp coaching calls that provide accountability and connection with our community members. They are a real game-changer because you can bring your field experiences onto the call and get coaching to perfect your sales process and increase your income.

Step 3 is much easier than Step 1. In Step 3, you'll make money if you've followed each step carefully. In fact, your client might even ask you for the sale. Excited? Let's move onto Chapter 17.

"How many no's am I willing to accept on my way to success?"

— Tom Hopkins, *How to Master the Art of Selling*

♡

CHAPTER 17

Waltzing Into Step Three

This is our last step in the 3 Step Sales Waltz™. Now it's time for you to make money. You've already done all of the heavy lifting in Steps 1 and 2. Let's get Julia back on Skype so I can show you how to guide your client through the last step.

"Hi, Julia. It's great to see you again. How's it going?"

"Good. Thanks for asking. How are things with you, Shirlene?"

"I can't believe how fast this week has passed. I gave you a lot to think over, didn't I? Were you able to find a job to relieve your money stress?"

"Not yet, but I'm looking. I've got some good prospects."

I now address Julia's Step 2 concerns and let her fill me in. I listen carefully and resist the impulses to sell or attempt to convince her to move forward. I avoid being pushy at all costs because the cost will be the loss of the client.

"Have you had a chance to think about how you might define your target market so you'll know how to speak to prospects to make an income?"

"I don't even know where to begin with that process, but I've thought a lot about it. I'm pretty much focusing on getting the job, and then I can think more clearly about my business. I'm not ready to take that step yet."

"Okay. No worries. I'm glad you let me know. I really appreciate the personal information you shared with me, and I know you'll be ready when you decide it's time to begin making the sales that support you. Can we check back again in another week?"

"Maybe two weeks might be better. Is that okay?"

"Sure. Let's get it on the calendar. How about Wednesday at 11:00 Pacific in two weeks? Does that work for you?"

"That works. See you then."

"Happy job hunting. I'll put some great energy out there for you in hopes that you'll manifest your new job quickly. I can't wait to see you get your first big sale. See you in two weeks. Bye-bye."

"Bye, Shirlene. I'll let you know if I get a job, and then we can move the appointment up. I'd like to get into your next two-day intensive."

"Great. I'll send the info about the course to your email. Oh, and by the way, would you like to receive my free weekly tips on business, finance, and sales?"

"That would be awesome. Please get me on that list right away. See you later, Shirlene. I look forward to talking to you again."

No matter how the conversation goes, you must remain calm. Have you ever heard the bullfrog theory? If not, here's how it goes:

> A bullfrog is sitting in a frying pan. The heat is on very low and the bullfrog is thinking, *Hmmm, this is nice and warm and it feels really good. I could stay here forever.* But then

someone gets the bright idea that if this is so comfy for the bullfrog, turning up the heat would be even better.

Yikes! the bullfrog thinks instantly. *I'm burning up.* And he jumps out of the pan. It's the same way with your prospect. Keep the heat on low and she'll be your friend and client forever. Turn up the heat and she'll give you a dirty look, jump out, hop away, and be gone forever. Lesson learned: Keep the heat on a warm simmer mixed with kindness, caring, and a heartfelt connection.

It's been two weeks now and Julia is expecting us. It's important to keep our agreement and show up on time. This enhances credibility and maintains relationship integrity.

And so the waltz begins….

"Hi, Julia. Long time no see. Got any news for me?"

"I do have news for you. I got a job, but I don't like it. It's miserable, and I can't wait to get back to working on my business. I hate being told what to do."

"Does that mean you'll be able to attend the next two-day intensive?"

"It does, but I'm going to have to call in sick. What are the hours?"

"It's 9 a.m. to 6 p.m. on both days. Want me to sign you up?"

"Yes, let's do it."

"Okay. Which credit card would you like to use?"

"I'll use my Visa card."

And that's all there is to the close. Julia already knew what she wanted and planned the next step toward her sales success. All she needed to do was resolve her personal challenge so she could relax into learning something new about her business. If I'd gotten upset or discouraged, Julia would have backed away, dropping me like a hot potato, and all of the trust we had previously built would have vanished instantly.

Yahoo! We just made a sale. Don't forget to celebrate.

EVALUATING YOUR 3 STEP SALES WALTZ™

Each time you waltz through the sales process, write down what you did right and what you could have done better. The following form can be downloaded at ShirleneReeves.com.

EVALUATING YOUR 3 STEP SALES WALTZ™

My Sales Evaluation for _____

Which personality type was I working with? Describe why you believe the person fit the personality type you chose. _____

_____

_____

_____

What information did I provide to fit this personality type? _____

_____

_____

_____

What could I have done better? _____

_____

_____

_____

Did I get impatient and leap to sell too quickly when my prospect asked what I do during Step 1 or Step 2? If so, how did I get triggered? _____

_____

_____

_____

Did I get tricked into talking about me in Step 1 when I should have waited for Step 2? _____

_____

_____

_____

What did I offer as suggestions to support my new prospect during

Step 2? _____

_____

_____

_____

How would I rate my newly formed active listening skills?

Fair   Good   Needs Improvement   Excellent

Did I talk too much? _____

Was I supportive and understanding during the step 3? _____

Did I ask for the credit card and make the sale? _____
If not, why not? _____

_____

_____

Overall, on a scale of 1 to 10, with 10 being the highest and 1 indicating needs improvement, circle how you would rate your waltz with this client.

1   2   3   4   5   6   7   8   9   10

What should I focus on to improve next time?

_____

_____

_____

_____

Be honest with yourself. Evaluate each sales waltz and keep them all in one file. This way you will easily see, over time, how much you've improved as you plant more and more seeds and grow more and more income.

"Everything you want is on the other side of fear."

— Jack Canfield

♡

CHAPTER 18

Questions from My Students

Regarding the quote by Jack Canfield on the opposite page, "Everything you want is on the other side of fear," I would add, "All you have to do is ask for what you want and remain calm." Remaining calm is important. Think about all those movies where people are playing poker. You need to keep your poker face if you want to win the sales game. You can't appear pushy or needy or the prospect will lose confidence in you and disappear.

When we talk about the other side of fear, it means you must step through the fear to get what you want, so if asking for money is a challenge for you, now is the time to step through that fear to make an income. However, if you've taken the time to make a new friend and build trust, it's much easier to ask for the money.

Of course, no sales process advice is perfect or will fit every situation. Therefore, I'm going to share with you the four most common questions I receive after my students try to apply this sales process in the real world.

Question 1: What do I do if the client cancels the appointment, can't decide, or says no?

A person who can't decide or cancels is still thinking about what you are offering. He may require more information or perhaps he needs more time to do research. Maybe he wants to learn more about you and your products. Provide him with testimonials, brochures, statistics, guarantees, and at times, have him reach out to previous clients for more input during the decision-making process.

No worries. Simply give him more time or find out if he needs more information. Sometimes, the time just isn't right, yet. If he turns you down, ask, "Is it no for now or no forever?" If it's no forever, move on and shout into the air, "Next!"

This one person shouldn't be your only client. Every time you leave the office or your home, you have another opportunity to plant new seeds, and just like a garden, each seed grows independently. Some grow quickly and reap fruit faster while others take longer, but the fruit is really juicy when it finally ripens.

Remember, your clients are watching and evaluating your behavior every time they come in contact with you. They're saying to themselves, "I know I need to do this, but what if it doesn't work? It's a big investment, and I'm scared to lay out the money." I promise, if you've built value into your conversations with your clients, they will eventually call you and say, "I'm ready now."

"Don't quit and eventually you will win."

— Evander Holyfield

In the financial world, it sometimes takes a year before a client is ready to take the step that makes me money. Have patience, my friends! Just keep planting your seeds with Steps 1 and 2. I promise you Step 3 will eventually arrive, and then it's time to celebrate your great success. One time, I had a client who called me two years after our initial appointment.

Question 2: What should I say if the prospect says, "I don't have the money or I can't afford your programs right now?"

I hear this a lot even with my own clients. In response, I ask, "What would you do if you knew exactly how to win? If you knew for sure that this process would make a huge difference in your income, would you spend the money to find out how to do it?"

Frequently, these people have the money, but they're afraid of making a mistake, and sometimes, they don't believe they'll receive the benefits or can do what you're suggesting to create the benefits they desire.

Circle back to what your potential client told you he was challenged with in Step 1. Repeat his words back to him. "Remember when you said you're running to networking groups and paying for branding and networking and the money is almost gone? If you don't learn how to sell, you'll never be able to keep your business, and you love working in your business, don't you?"

Then paint the dream again with what if statements to remind your prospect how you will get him to the benefits he desires. "What if you were able to sell so well that you never had to worry about money again? I know you can do this. All you need are the steps to make the income flow into your bank account."

Question 3: My prospect told me she doesn't have the time to take my program. What should I say?

Ask her when she will have the time. For my two-day intensive, I tell prospects the date of the next course and suggest they carve out the time to attend. I also suggest that they can make payments and ask whether they'd like to make a deposit to save a seat in the next course.

When people say they don't have the time, they are simply making an excuse. All you need to do is find out why.

I always revert to my favorite statement, "If you knew exactly how to win and could start adding income to your checking account right now, would you be able to find the time?" How would you answer that question? You can always throw in a few additional bonuses that are so juicy that they can't refuse, but add them with the stipulation that they must act now.

Question 4: What tips can you give me for client retention?

This is a great question because conscientious client-retention techniques are vitally important to your business. Your clients are both your biggest fans and your greatest referral source.

If you make every effort to take excellent care of your prospects by meeting their needs, they'll become your clients forever. Many of my clients are like family, and in many cases, they're closer to me than family.

I find activities that we can do together, like walking on the beach, attending networking events together, or going to movies, concerts, book launches, and educational events. I also arrange for zoom trainings and additional events that provide visibility for them.

Most importantly, I answer the phone when they call, and I use their name in my greeting. I can't tell you how many say, "I can't believe you answered the phone. I'm so grateful you picked up." Those who answer the phone when it rings are rare. Be one of the rare business owners who cares about communicating with your clients. You will, for sure, stand out in the crowd.

"The goal as a company is to have customer service that is not just the best but legendary."

— Sam Walton, Founder of Wal-Mart

♡

CHAPTER 19

Generating Referrals and Client Retention

Although not everyone you speak to is the right client for you, it's still a positive move to listen carefully to what prospects have to say. You never know whom they know. If you are a kind, caring focused listener, others will appreciate that you took the time to get to know them for something other than a sale. As a result, they'll think of you when they run across someone who might need your product or service.

Referrals are the highest form of compliment you can receive because they mean you are top of mind in another's thoughts. The large corporations pay millions to achieve this goal, but you can do it even better as an individual and be much more efficient.

To receive referrals, you must be referable. This means you deliver what you promise. Not delivering means you have an upset, angry client who will share this knowledge with everyone he knows. In this day and age, not being referable is the biggest mistake you can make because it's so easy to spread the word through social media.

I have a great example for you. In October 2016, I hired a woman to coach me on building a Facebook funnel for the sale of my programs. In the process, she convinced me that I should change my entire website in the interest of looking more professional. Everyone loved my site, but it occurred to me that she might be right. Because she had just spoken at the Harvard School of Business, I was under the impression that her values and integrity were congruent with mine.

After her team reviewed my website and we decided on the pricing, we both signed a well-written contract (provided by her) that clearly stated all of the work would be completed in ten weeks. This included the transfer of the website into a new theme and the funnels being designed and loaded into Click Funnels. Then my marketing could move forward.

I signed a $4,800 check to comply with the contractual agreement for the work. She wouldn't allow payment on my credit card, which would have provided protection for me if the work didn't get completed on time.

In December 2016, I suggested that she be featured on the cover of my magazine. She said she also wanted to have a two-page spread in the magazine, but that she didn't have the money to pay for it and would reimburse me the following week. The magazine was developed; I covered her costs and massively marketed it, giving her the advantage of a huge amount of visibility, not knowing that she didn't intend to reimburse me.

Nine months later, the site and funnels still hadn't been completed, and as I write this, I still have not been reimbursed the $1,000 in costs for the magazine front cover and two-page spread.

Will I refer her? Absolutely not, and in fact, I have a large world-wide community that will never work with her as a result of how she treated me. I think you get the picture. If you have clients, you must treat them like gold. If you do, they will act as your mouthpiece and refer you at every opportunity. If you don't treat them well, the same mouthpiece will work in reverse, ruining your reputation.

HOW TO GET REFERRALS

If you work with business people, use LinkedIn. The funnels for me should never have been slated for Facebook because Facebook is for personal products and interactions, and my company is better suited for B2B connections on LinkedIn's Advanced People Search.

To interact on LinkedIn's Advanced People Search, go to "Advanced" next to the search bar at the top of the page, and then click "People" on the left-hand side of the screen. From there, you can filter your search by second-degree connections as well as additional specifics such as industry, title, keywords, and location to turn up a list of potential referral opportunities.

Once you find someone you'd like to connect with, hover over the arrow next to the "Connect" button and select "Get Introduced" from the menu.

This gives you the ability to choose a first-degree connection to introduce you. It's best to create a quick message for that person about why you'd like to be introduced.

VIDEO TESTIMONIALS = REFERRAL OPPORTUNITIES

Another way to get referrals is to complete the work you've been contracted for and then ask for a video testimonial to put on your website. This is easy to do on Zoom. It's free to sign up for a Zoom account, and once you click the "Start a Meeting" button, you'll get a new meeting number that you can give to your client. When the client appears on screen, check the lighting so she will show up well-lit. Don't click the record button until you've provided some preparation on what you want the client to say. You don't want every customer to say the same thing, and the customer will always appreciate a tip and some direction on what will work best for you.

After completing the video, you can ask whether the customer might know of someone interested in the same service she just received. When you ask this question, narrow down how your customer might know this person. You could say, "Do you know someone at your church?" or "Do you know someone at your school?" The reason you narrow it down is so that a person's brain can focus in on a specific place rather than be searching everyone she knows. If you don't narrow it down, you'll probably get a no.

EMAILING FOR REFERRALS

Help your clients out if you want email referrals because they really have no idea what to say or how to address someone else when it comes to referring you. I've provided an easy template that you can use.

> Hi [Referral],
>
> I'm not sure whether I've mentioned this in the past, but I've been working with [your name] for a few months. The other day, I was talking with her about some of the things we had done together, and it suddenly occurred to me that I should introduce the two of you. So...
>
> [Referral], meet [your name, with a LinkedIn or FB profile URL].

[your name], meet [Referral, with a LinkedIn or FB profile URL].

Now I leave it to the two of you.

I look forward to chatting with you both later.

After sending this email template, you can check in a week or two later with your customer to see whether she had an opportunity to connect with anyone who might be interested in your services. If she didn't, let it go.

PROVIDING AMAZING SERVICE

If you want referrals, it's important to follow up as promised, answer the phone when people call, use your focused listening skills, and never ever deal with a complaint over text. If there's a problem, pick up the phone immediately and do whatever you can to resolve it as efficiently as possible. If it's your fault, bend over backwards to keep your client happy. Give lots of bonuses. A happy client will always make you happy with referrals.

PART THREE

MARKETING WITH MASSIVE VISIBILITY

"Good marketing makes the company look smart. Great marketing makes the customer feel smart."

— Joe Chernov

♡

CHAPTER 20

Stepping Into Leadership and Visibility

In today's world, the bigger your visibility worldwide, the more credible you become. I believe that if you're willing to play a bigger game, more souls will benefit from your vast experience and knowledge.

Years ago, Oprah brought this theory to light. Before she featured Dr. Oz, Suze Orman, and Dr. Phil, no one even knew who they were, but now look at them. Simply because they were featured on *The Oprah Winfrey Show*, everyone believes they are the "go-to" experts in their fields of expertise. This is why I say, "Sell yourself, not your product."

The trick to achieving massive credibility is to stand out and maintain consistent visibility until people see you so often that they begin to believe you. You'll know this has occurred when they say, "I see you everywhere." Many of my students have heard this exact comment from people they see at networking events. I frequently have people who walk up to me and say, "I know you from somewhere, but I can't seem to place you." I know why they know me. It's because I'm massively visible on the worldwide web. The trick is to stay in front of your prospect weekly and forget identifying yourself with phrases like "The Best," "Number One," or "The Biggest." No one believes it anyway, and it doesn't increase your credibility. Know that the more frequently you are seen, the better your chances are for client responses.

There was a time when only those hand-picked by the media could make an impression on a syndicated TV station, but now we all have an opportunity to step up. The world will listen and believe if we appear to be professional and share a credible message, but you have to be unique and different from your competition. Ask yourself, "What makes me stand out that will attract attention in the marketplace?" Think about what you might know that's different. Is your character one that you can promote? Most of all, you must put integrity first so your clients will trust and refer you. Write down how you are different from your competition. If you aren't clear about how to answer this question, do some research on the web. Determine who your competition is and what they provide. How are you different from your competition? (Example: better service, unique positioning and knowledge, etc.)

People buy you first, your benefits second, and then your company, so why lead with your company name? Use personal videos as much as possible. Take a look at my website and you'll see a video message from me on almost every page. I want prospects to get to know me. The more you get to know me through my videos, the more you'll trust me. In this way, we build a relationship toward working together. To give you an example, I'll give you a list of how I'm different.

- Every week, I send out a two-minute video blog with an important tip and a do-today takeaway. I address the email to each individual, using his or her name. I never want my prospects or clients to feel like they're a number in my database. I appreciate them as individuals and know each one of them personally.
- I have 400+ videos on my YouTube channel at http://www.youtube.com/c/ShirleneReeves.
- All of my blogs relate to each other, and when you click on one, it's on my playlist so it's easy to watch one right after the next.
- I'm interviewed weekly on one or more web TV shows, podcasts, or radio shows.
- I use press releases for upcoming events that make me stand out.
- I wrote the book *Selling Through Your Heart.*
- I'm a keynote speaker who travels worldwide.
- I write articles and post them on four LinkedIn groups.
- I have video testimonials from my students on my course web pages.
- My LinkedIn page is up-to-date. It includes videos, and I post my badge on my site: https://www.linkedin.com/in/shirlenereeves/.
- I created a Facebook community called Massive Visibility

Entrepreneurs where I post regularly: https://www.facebook.com/groups/MassiveVisibilityEntrepreneurs/.

- I've hosted a web TV show called *WMAX.TV* with twenty-six thirty-minute episodes that have been broadcasted on Voice America TV and that are now on my website.

- I host a syndicated radio show live called *Ascended Masters at Work* that is uploaded weekly to iTunes and marketed on social media: https://bbsradio.com/ascendedmastersatwork.

Now it's your turn to write down what you are currently doing to stand out in your marketplace.

LEADING THROUGH VISIBILITY

If you want to become a visible "go-to" guest expert, you need to appear as a credible, believable leader, who speaks with good purpose. This allows others to feel comfortable and confident in following you. It's important that you be a good listener who is connected to intuitive guidance and, at the very least, appears to be grounded and calm under pressure.

Emotional control and fear become the biggest challenges when stepping onto stages, into the lights on a TV set, or being interviewed on radio. You must never forget that others are watching and listening to how skillfully you deliver the information you provide.

There are few true leaders in our society, and most people are followers looking for leaders who relate to their thought processes and values. Mastering the skills of leadership is highly valued because so few have accomplished the identifiable traits needed to step into the lights.

According to the Center for American Progress, women make up the majority of the US population. They earn approximately 60 percent of undergraduate degrees, 60 percent of all master's degrees, and 44 percent of the master's degrees in business and management. Although they hold almost 52 percent of all professional-level jobs, American women lag substantially behind men when it comes to their representation in leadership positions. While they are 45 percent of the overall S&P 500 labor force and 37 percent of first or mid-level officials and managers in those companies, they are only 25 percent of executive- and senior-level officials and managers, hold only 19 percent of board seats, and are only 4.6 percent of CEOs. (This paragraph was written specifically for the High Cs. Can you guess why?)

It may surprise you to know that without women in the workplace, we couldn't have won World War II. Women have always been an integral part of the US economic workforce.

My purpose here on earth is to lift and support large communities of women entrepreneurs looking for the answers to leadership and how to become visible in their marketplaces through media so they can speak their purposes and accomplish their missions worldwide. Most of these women are living in the second chapter of their lives and have held substantial positions in Fortune 500 companies for, in some cases, as many as twenty-three years. Many have been laid off in favor of younger generation employees who are working for less pay and lower medical premiums.

Many of these women are at the time in their lives when they may choose to enter the entrepreneurial world. Doing so usually means it's time for them to shine. A myriad of women's groups exist to provide support and encouragement. Frequently, their biggest question is: "I have so many skills that I don't know how to pull it all together into one business. How do I define what I do?"

These women come from all backgrounds, and they make excellent speakers and leaders because of their ease in connecting to their audiences. In a room of mostly women, there is no quality more valuable and endearing than creating a connection with the audience.

Women are often intuitive and can easily relate well to their audiences while building trust and creating acceptance. After years of child-rearing, they are amazing storytellers, and they have excellent skills when it comes to painting the dream of the benefits provided by their businesses.

For these reasons, I enjoy guiding women forward by assisting them in building confidence, creating focused presentations, and developing properly priced programs that lead other women into their next steps and dreams, thereby lifting whole communities.

However, stepping into this big shift can be challenging for many women because they have been leaders in the corporate world, but they have no idea how to work within the parameters of the entrepreneurial genre. They are required to use a different language, behave differently, and show up differently, plus they are literally on their own in adjusting to a new feeling of loneliness never before experienced.

RECOGNIZING YOU AS A LEADER

This new world is all about self-awareness, self-regulation, and self-motivation. Each of these traits is important, so I want to look at each one in more detail. As you read through them, you might find that some aspects of each trait you've already accomplished while others may require more work.

Self-Awareness

Forbes determined that, "a high self-awareness score was the strongest predictor of overall success." This isn't surprising since executives usually understand where their weaknesses appear and then hire subordinates who are able to perform well in those categories. These leaders are also better able to entertain the idea that someone on their team may have an idea that is even better than their own. Finally, self-aware leaders have an understanding of how their words and feelings affect those around them.

Self-Regulation

Here is where we talk about having control of your emotions and actions. An awareness of your personal values and how accountable you hold yourself when you make golden mistakes will determine your success as a leader.

Our emotions are driven by biological impulses. These impulses frequently get beyond our control, but what happens as a result of these emotions is not. When our emotions ratchet out of control, it's impossible to ignore them, but we can take care to manage them carefully. Emotional management is called self-regulation, and it's the emotional intelligence quality that allows us to avoid uncontrolled emotional outbursts.

A person who knows how to self-regulate possesses:

- Thoughtful consideration before reacting impulsively

- The ability to accept change and then go with the flow of inner guidance

- Integrity around the ability to say no to impulsive urges and follow through as agreed. In other words, she will do what she says she'll do.

Self-Motivation

Self-motivation seems to be one of the most difficult challenges entrepreneurs are required to manage. For the most part, they are alone in their work, which creates impulses to do anything but work and stay focused on the tasks required to turn a baby business into a booming income-generating enterprise. Often, my students will claim they couldn't do their homework assignments because family got in the way, they were tired, a pet went to the vet, etc. I've heard it all, and I always say, "Whether you do or you don't work, you have free will. It's entirely up to you."

Lack of motivation often sets into motion a never-ending stream of negative self-talk. Over time, the stress of lack of income begins to rear its ugly head, creating chaos in your checkbook. Doing what needs to be done when it needs to be done is the fastest way to replace nagging negativity with power and positivity.

Here are a few ideas to help you stay self-motivated and focused on your tasks:

Networking: Being around others, in your correctly defined target market, will assist in keeping you motivated at higher levels. Attending conferences, seminars, and workshops are a great way to recharge your batteries.

Being Accountable: To stay self-motivated as a leader, find a trusted friend or reach out to your coach and ask him or her to help you stay on track with the specific projects or goals you're working on. Knowing you'll need to report to someone can often give you that extra energy you need to get things done. For the same reason, it's advisable to provide a weekly follow-up group call or mastermind community after teaching your programs. Students do their best to take notes and process your teachings during the course, but they can't remember everything. Group calls allow for re-teaching and better understanding through focused accountability.

Staying Focused: While working your way through accomplishing your goals, keep them visible. Visibility makes it easier to stay motivated; it reminds you of why you chose to become an entrepreneur.

The easiest way to keep your goals visible is to find a picture of your dream and place it on your refrigerator so you see it every time you walk by or open the door. This picture serves two purposes: 1) It keeps you focused on your goals, and 2) It reminds you to keep moving forward toward your goals.

Exercising and Taking Breaks: Try not to sit too long, and take long walks. Fitness may not seem important, but taking care of your physical needs with movement builds energy and will assist you in staying motivated. I'd like to add a comment here about the importance of your health. You've been told before that you must take care of yourself before you can take care of others; however, I've watched as powerful business owners who aren't able to stop running soon create a negative affect on their health. There may be only you out there looking after your business, but keep in mind that without your good health, there will be no business to manage.

Getting Away from the TV: The television sucks in more entrepreneurs than any other distraction. Stay off the couch or turn off network programming like I did. On Demand was my biggest challenge. So many programs got recorded that I would spend hours staring at the boob tube trying to catch up with all of my recorded programming.

Then one day I woke up to the fact that I wasn't required to watch all of those programs, so I canceled the cable. It was truly a freeing experience, and the benefit is that the feeling of getting behind no longer exists because I set deadlines for completion of my work that I can easily meet as a result of no longer wasting time in an effort to catch up on pre-recorded TV shows. Better yet, not having cable saved me approximately $1,440 per year and you can save like this too, depending on your current cable package.

Exhibiting Empathy: Empathy is more than sympathy, which is being able to understand and support others with compassion or sensitivity. Empathy is the ability to experience and relate to the thoughts, emotions, and experiences of others. Empathy is fundamental to leadership.

Empathetic leaders rarely speak. They concentrate on practicing focused listening skills. Today, so many distractions surround us that we are significantly impacted by the quality of our listening skills. An empathetic leader will turn off and put away her cell phone, shut down her email, and focus her attention on the individual sitting in front of her.

Empathetic leaders are also non-judgmental, even when sensing that others' feelings are in direct conflict with their own. They sincerely appreciate what the other person is experiencing and understand how those feelings are affecting that person's perception and decision-making process.

Lastly, an empathetic leader displays emotional intelligence. She has the ability to step back from her own agenda, and the other person's feelings, to evaluate and analyze those feelings in a subjective manner. Empathetic leaders don't let the feelings involved in a situation control the outcome.

MASTERING SOCIAL LEADERSHIP SKILLS

Social skills are key components of social intelligence. They include the ability to express oneself in social interactions; the ability to "read" and understand different social situations; and an understanding of social roles, norms, problem-solving skills, and social role-playing skills.

Being challenged by these key components of social skills can make a world of difference in how you show up in the business arena. Once you review them, you'll find that if you are lacking in or unaware of the meaning of these non-verbal cues, you can quickly and easily make the shifts necessary for increased leadership impact.

Becoming acutely aware of and sensitive to non-verbal cues of all kinds is difficult because we are all overwhelmed with digital communication. However, to interpret body language (non-verbal cues) effectively in face-to-face interactions, you must be able to recognize your thought processes and how they relate to facial expressions and body language. This means it's important to shut-off the noise in your head long enough to read other people's cues and understand what's going on inside their heads.

How important is body language? Actually, only 7 percent of our communication comes through speaking. In 1971, Albert Mehrabian published *Silent Messages*, in which he discussed his research on non-verbal communication. He concluded that:

> Prospects based their assessments of credibility on factors other than the words the salesperson spoke—the prospects studied assigned 55 percent of their weight to the speaker's body language and another 38 percent to the tone and music of their voice. They assigned only 7 percent of their credibility assessment to the salesperson's actual words.

These statistics tell us that it's important to be aware of how we show up at all times because we're judged within the first few seconds of meeting someone. That means leaders must master the five social leadership skills and become self-aware on all levels of communication. Those five skills are:

1. **Handshaking:** Your handshake speaks volumes. What message do you want to convey about yourself? In order for people to believe you are strong, confident, and self-assured, shake people's hands firmly with confidence and look them in the eye with a smile. This will instantly begin to build trust and start your conversation off in a positive manner.

2. **Sitting up straight and standing tall:** While interviewing on radio, TV, or Zoom, sit up straight, on the front half of your chair, and engage with your host and the camera. Let the energy of your body fill the space so you look and feel like a leader. When you sit or stand with your shoulders back, opening up your chest, you are able to communicate with a commanding presence before even uttering your first words.

3. **Interacting regularly:** Interaction gives you an opportunity to know and understand what your clients are thinking as well as how they are feeling and reacting to your thoughts and pre-

sentations. This means that when engaging with others proactively—even if in a digital format—you can build a cohesive community with brand recognition. By reaching out early and often, you'll learn valuable insights that you'd never anticipate otherwise.

4. **Openly discussing your values and purpose:** People join communities for many reasons, but what's more interesting is why they stay. They stay connected because they feel a sense of shared values, purpose, mission, and vision. If you're a leader, it's imperative that you regularly reinforce your values and purpose.

5. **Encouraging a community presence:** Social media is vital in an entrepreneur's world. It's one of the few ways we stay connected to our clients and build a referral base. Providing Zoom mastermind groups, online events, compelling free calls, weekly video blogging email tips, and frequent texting are all part of encouraging a community presence. A good leader watches his community carefully to make sure no entrepreneur gets left behind and that all are included or at the very least aware of important upcoming events.

6. **Demonstrating authentic interest in every community member:** Sincerity and authenticity make the difference between a leader and a task manager. If you're not sincere, you'll do things that might make business sense, but eventually, they'll boomerang and hurt others. Always think before you act while demonstrating heartfelt leadership skills with kindness and caring. If one of your community members is upset, take the time to pick up the phone and listen carefully before speaking. An unhappy member can be the start of a cancer that ruins an entire membership.

When considering a new client or accepting a new entrepreneur into your community, take the time to meet with him or her in person, on Skype, or over the phone. It's imperative that each person in your community believes in and maintains the values of the group in order to build a cohesive organization that supports each member in an effort to build and lift all the businesses together.

About a month ago, I set an appointment with a potential client who was interested in becoming a "go-to" guest expert in her area of expertise. My clients hire me for life, so it's very important that we are able to communicate and work together efficiently. During the preliminary steps to deciding whether a person is a good "media presence" candidate for representing her area of expertise, I find it highly effective to observe how the participant builds a working relationship. Two of my major core values are integrity and mutual respect. In the scenario below, let's see what happens when I take these preliminary steps with a candidate we'll call Ann.

Here is what I experienced with Ann in our preliminary meeting:

> I called, and texted Ann, one hour prior to our scheduled meeting time to confirm.

> My message went to voicemail and there was no answer to my text. I had no clarity on whether Ann would arrive to meet with me.

> I arrived at the previously agreed upon place on time and waited ten minutes before Ann arrived with excuses and a flippant "Sorry about that."

> During our twenty minutes together, Ann checked her cell phone three times, asking me to wait while she responded to her text messages. It seemed odd that she would be so diligent with her text responses when she hadn't returned my confirmation text. I was feeling disrespected because I believe leaders should set their phones to silent mode and put them away, while providing undivided attention and respect to others taking the time to meet with them.

During the few remaining minutes, Ann would ask good questions, but during my answers, her eyes would drift out the window when something caught her attention. I could see she wasn't focused on what I was saying.

At the close of our remaining twenty minutes, I told Ann I had another appointment and would need to leave to be on time for my next client. She whined and complained that I didn't give her enough time to get all of her questions answered. I politely responded by saying, "I think you might be too busy to take on a media presence at this time."

Would I choose Ann as my client? No! Her behavior spoke volumes about the importance of our meeting. Her tardiness without calling to inform me she would be late, her checking her phone, and her aloof apology violated my core values. She did not respect my time, and her integrity was questionable. If she arrived late and distracted when meeting me, she would be late for a TV show or radio interview.

When someone takes the time and makes the effort to connect with you, give that person the respect she deserves. You never know what the benefits of this meeting might provide, and treating others as though their time isn't valuable hurts your integrity and a reputation that is costly to build.

My students are frequently given assignments that involve working together with other community members in an effort to reach their desired goals. Experiencing what it means to follow through, while respecting each other's time, and while meeting the five social leadership skills makes an incredible difference in how far you climb the entrepreneurial ladder.

Each member in a community takes responsibility for providing accountability and creates opportunities to connect with other community members, thereby establishing referral relationships while building confidence and support among community members.

Developing an understanding of what it means to become a leader, and then stepping into the role, with a professional air of confidence, makes a big difference in how your clients perceive you and your credibility.

USING BOOKS TO BUILD CREDIBILITY

Properly written books can be parlayed into amazing integrity-building tools for massive visibility. A book is a multi-purpose marketing instrument that can provide you with a great deal of attention, authority, and credibility. Most people won't take a risk that sets them up to be judged because it displays to the world what they know or don't know. However, if you are willing to step into taking that risk, you'll become the "go-to" expert in your area of expertise. Having a great book brings your clients toward you.

A well-written book defines who you are as a business owner and provides clarity on how you support your clients. There is no better foundational tool for building your brand and attracting new clients.

Writing a chapter in a book does not provide the same benefits and frequently ends up under your bed because books by multiple authors are difficult to sell. When your professional integrity is represented only as a chapter in a book, even if you are pictured on the front cover, it doesn't deliver the same oomph as a book written fully by your own creative genius.

Many entrepreneurs tell me they buy into contributing a chapter in an anthology because they want to be titled as a published author, but what good is a book with other contributors who don't write as well as you do? These manuscripts are often painful to read, there is no gel in the content, and while some chapters are penned well, others are not. The editing frequently leaves a great deal to be desired, and you rarely have control over what happens to the book after it's published. I usually leave such books in the seat pocket of the plane when I depart.

BOOK MARKETING MISTAKES

Nothing is sadder than watching an entrepreneur who spent months writing her own book and paid for expensive editing and production costs decide that what she needs to do to "get it out there" is sign up with a marketing firm. So she plunks down $20,000 and signs a contract with a marketing firm that promises to get her speaking engagements and interviews on the radio and network TV.

Next, off the author goes, flying from one city to the next, paying for hotel rooms and expensive meals in an effort to keep up with the marketing firm's promised agenda. If this sounds good to you, OUCH! Let me rip off the Band-Aid and expose the reasons why this marketing ploy doesn't increase your income. Splattering information about your book on massive amounts of people who may or may not be in your target market is a waste of money.

Not knowing what to say or showing up on camera in a way that doesn't relate to your clients is a waste of time and hard-earned money. It usually doesn't take long before these dreamers begin to feel the pain of exhaustion and burnout from trying to keep up with the rigorous schedule of the book signing tour.

Recently, I watched as one entrepreneur wrote her $20,000 check, handed it to the marketing company, and then spent another $10,000 flying all over the United States to appear on radio and TV shows. I attended her book-signing launch and watched as six months of her campaign slipped quickly by with no results. It was a complete bust, and now she is miserable selling for an MLM and still paying small amounts on a big monthly 17 percent credit card bill.

If you've written a book, congratulations! It takes a lot of dedicated time, discipline, and focus. But don't try to turn a fifty-page ebook into a national bestseller. No amount of money can do that. Instead, important strategies and plans must be built in and around your work that include social networking, driving clients to your website, and providing weekly videos or blogs talking about what's inside your book, why it will benefit a well-defined target market, and where potential clients can buy it.

Patrick Snow, known for his talents in author development, keynote speaking, and publishing programs, says that books are your calling card for advancing in the arena of keynote speaking. He suggests that to be selected for keynote speaking opportunities, your book should contain 50,000 to 60,000 words, be 200 to 300 pages, and have an outrageously professional eye-catching cover. And that's just the beginning of the journey. Creating a book gives you instant credibility as a powerful thought leader.

When you take the role of an authentic leader who is open, honest, and credible, others see your value and a community of caring, kind, heartfelt individuals comes together. Always lead by example and others will follow your goodwill. The more visible you are, the more you will be respected and lifted by other thought leaders who have written books and put themselves out into the world in a way that makes a difference to millions.

That's what I call getting out of your own backyard, and it all starts with becoming a celebrity guest expert, representing your specific area of expertise, and it's time to get you started on that path right now.

"People live in the shadows of people instead of standing on the shoulders of giants and releasing the giant within."

— Dr. John Demartini

♡

CHAPTER 21

Becoming a Celebrity Guest Expert

Live streaming has become a thing of the present while network TV is dwindling in numbers to a thing of the past. Those who dropped the traditional programming packages have moved to big names like Netflix, Hulu, Amazon TV, Roku, Apple TV, and a number of others where they can select commercial-free, quality programming.

Did you know that Netflix's *House of Cards* received fourteen primetime Emmy award-winning nominations? Right now, Web TV is in its infancy, so there are very few shows on the web and even fewer guest experts who pack a professional punch. But did you know that this year 89 million people will be watching 1.2 billion videos online and cross-platform consumers are more than twice as likely as TV-only viewers to use social networking to discover new programs? Will your videos be in the running?

Now that you've completed the exercises in the previous chapters, your foundation has been laid to become a professional celebrity guest expert. You are now armed with the first steps toward massive visibility. What if you could increase your income, move your business to the next level, and become the "go-to" guest expert in your specialized area of expertise?

When it comes to sales, massive visibility is the only way to go. People have to know who you are and what you're all about if you want to make more money. Just like you, I got tired of playing in my own backyard and making an insignificant income.

Believe me; it wasn't about being able to sell. It was about whom I was attempting to sell to. I desperately needed a bigger pool to play in, and I bet you're ready to swim in the deep end too. The question is: Are you ready to learn the secrets to becoming massively visible and stop struggling in the kiddie pool?

Can you imagine what it's like to be pursued, rather than constantly running in pursuit of your clients? What if people said to you, like they say to me, "I see you everywhere. How do you do it?" when in reality I spend most of my time in the comfort of my own home studio.

Imagine what it might feel like to relax, get out of the traffic, and send the majority of your professional messaging out over the web while selecting only the largest and most influential networking groups and events to attend once a month.

Now that you have a defined target market and you speak their language, life becomes a great deal easier. The opportunities are monumental and you'll find that you can pick and choose wisely, which will enable you to connect with new individuals who can introduce you into groups of highly qualified communities.

Becoming an expert in your own home studio saves a great deal of money. You no longer are required to rent rooms in hotels for events, pay videographers thousands of dollars to do little video recordings, or hunt for paid stages to speak on. If you learn to use YouTube and YouTube live-streaming feature, you'll soar to the top of the Google rankings.

We are on the cutting edge of Web TV, and those of us in this arena are actually *making history*. Can you believe it? We're like Steve Jobs and Bill Gates when they invented the first computers. The web isn't monitored, so we can speak openly and be truthful about our messages and what we find important to share with the public.

These are exciting times—video blogs are broadcasting on every platform, but there are many platforms you haven't even thought about yet. There are the:

- **Food monitors:** You've seen those big monitors in restaurants and bars.

- **Grocery store monitors:** Costco has monitors everywhere when you walk in the front door. Wouldn't it be awesome to see your own video on the biggest monitor the store's got?

- **Gas tank monitors:** These provide mini-commercials while drivers fill up their tanks. All it takes is a three-minute sound bite of awareness for someone to follow up on your message.

Zoom, Skype, Facebook live streaming, and YouTube have changed the way we do business. Within the last few years, television viewers made a huge switch to streaming Web TV and dropped their network programming. They say they've grown tired of being dumbed down by commercial airtime and shopping networks in favor of quality programming.

Producing a show on Web TV is pro-active marketing. You're not waiting for something to happen. You're stepping up to make it happen. What if 140,000 people could see you while you sit in your personal studio sharing your message? That's an awesome thought, isn't it?

That's what happened to me when I was on a web reality show for fourteen weeks. The show's intention was to teach nine panelists how to turn their own TV shows into cash, but my intention was very different. A week before the show host called, I had an intuitive knowing that I needed to become massively visible on web TV. I knew that joining the show would launch me onto a platform where I could speak on the importance of understanding easy financial principles to enhance global knowledge, lift public awareness, and enhance the economy. When the show host called, I instinctively knew it was the next step in my mission and business growth.

Seven panelists and I learned how to show up massively, develop a set, light it properly, and step into becoming an guest expert in our specific fields. My very first set was actually in my garage, sandwiched between the garbage cans and my car, with a room divider behind me. For fourteen weeks, in three-hour segments, I climbed into my chair shrouded by darkness until I switched on the lighting that made my 4x4 set beam like a professional studio.

At the time, it felt like I was alone, working with seven other panelists who appeared on the show with me. We were all in the learning process, making crazy mistakes, laughing at ourselves, and openly expressing our technological frustrations. As the weeks wore on, we got better, our confidence grew, and it didn't take long to begin presenting ourselves professionally.

During the filming, I gave no thought to the fact that others might be watching me joke around, laughing at myself, and probably not coming off as seriously as I should have. In any case it was fun and memorable, so much so that I teach my students how to reenact this experience in my Massive Visibility Media™ courses and they love it. I did, ultimately, have my own web TV show, but I never could figure out how to turn it into cash. Fortunately, the show broke even and my co-host and I each walked away with $1,000 when it was all said and done.

It wasn't until the show was over, and we all met at the Burbank Media Center, that I discovered it wasn't only the members on the panel who were present. It was a long drive from Northern California to reach the studio, so I thought I'd slip in quietly to meet the other panel members. We were all old friends by that time, and I was looking forward to connecting in person. Instead, viewers had flown in from all over the world to meet us. Imagine my surprise when I walked in the door and had people rush toward me saying, "Shirlene, you are my favorite. You are so much fun." They pulled me over to snap photos and begged me to go to dinner with them.

This was the first time I truly felt like a celebrity guest expert. I had no idea that so many fans were watching me broadcast from a tiny space that looked to them like a professional studio. I quickly learned the power of massive visibility on the web and how it could easily impact a global audience.

SELLING OUTSIDE YOUR OWN BACKYARD

These are exciting times with big opportunities for leaping out of our own backyard and making a massive difference in the world. Since Web TV is in its infancy, it's great for coaches and entrepreneurs because we don't have much competition.

When I started WMAX.TV, with my co-host Barbara Wainwright, there were very few professional guest experts to interview, so I developed the Massive Visibility Media™ courses to teach entrepreneurs how to show up confidently and "celebrity ready" for their interviews.

The show was recorded on a set with four-time Emmy award-winning director Richard Crawford in San Diego County. There was no time to train entrepreneurs who had no idea what it meant to show up professionally, speak in three-minute sound bites, or carry on a conversation that would be interesting to a television audience. Aside from this challenge, the costs incurred on the set were astronomical, so Barbara and I devised a system to shoot five shows in six hours. Our contract with Voice America TV obligated us to twenty-six weeks of twenty-eight-minute shows.

Each show included two guests with fifteen minutes of interview time on the set. We were one-shot wonders with great synergy. This meant that we interviewed as many as ten guests in one afternoon with only one take each. We have twenty-six shows full of amazing enlightening interviews with such greats as Robert G. Allen, Dr. John Demartini, Bob Donnell, Steve Farber. and Dr. Nick Delgado. Visit my website if you'd like to see them at ShirleneReeves.com.

QUALITIES THAT SHOW HOSTS LOOK FOR

When you become a celebrity guest expert, you become highly sought-after in the media world. The show hosts know you've been trained to show up professionally, and you interview in a way that makes them look phenomenal.

- You know what it means to show up "celebrity ready" with the proper makeup that makes you look like a star under the bright lights.

- You know instantly how to relax your show host and make him or her sparkle with enthusiasm so you receive repeat interviews.

- You're armed with the secrets to impact audiences, draw in your clients, and make sales.

- You speak in three-minute sound bites that pack a punch.

- You've boiled down the explanation of your business to five to seven words.

- You're confident about sharing your finely tuned thirty-second promo during networking group introductions, during media interviews, and while connecting one-on-one with potential clients.

- You show up in the green room on time in an attire that avoids video pixilation.

- You've stood on the red carpet and presented who you are to the world, and you now use that two-minute video on your email signature line, your website, and as an introduction for speaking engagements.

- You are comfortable, prepared, and confident with a big smile and heartfelt engagement.

If you're an entrepreneur looking for the answer to making a difference in the world and your business, you might be ready to become a celebrity guest expert on Web TV and step into massive visibility. Nothing is more expensive than a missed opportunity.

SPEAKING FROM THE STAGE

"I speak from the stage, but no one buys. It doesn't matter how long I rehearse."

This is a big complaint from all of my incoming students. Why? It's because they believe that when they speak, they can sell everyone, but the reality is that we're not meant to support everyone, and it's virtually impossible to boil down your verbiage to a target market so vast. It's more productive to pinpoint your audience and then define the words and phrases that audience is waiting to hear. If you established your target market and did the exercise in Chapter 8 that provides for the words and phrases your clients are waiting to hear, your speech will be much more powerful and you will get sales when you step down from the stage. All you need to do now is add those words into your speeches where they can elicit the most impact.

Here's an example to illustrate my point: I had a student who was trying to do business in both the corporate and entrepreneurial worlds. When she spoke on stages, her speeches were designed to reach both groups. Consequently, she got no sales results. Once we refined her speeches to be directed toward the audience she had pinpointed for a specific event, it made a world of difference in her income. Now she's so busy speaking and supporting her clients that it's almost impossible to connect with her for coffee.

Believe it or not, there was a time when I was terrified of speaking on stage. I was extremely shy, and I've always been a bit of an introvert. But you'd never know it when I step into the lights, and it's all because of Toastmasters, the international organization that teaches you how to become an effective speaker. In 1995, I earned the Distinguished Toastmaster Designation. Toastmasters has taken me a long way in my career, and it will do the same for you. It's a great place to practice and refine your sales speeches too. I'll talk more about it in a minute.

FINDING VISIBILITY OPPORTUNITIES

Once your programs are developed and priced properly, in a way that will attract your target market, it's time to step into massive visibility. You'll be amazed by how many opportunities show up when you're ready to step up. I'll mention a few here, but there's so much more that it would take a whole book to list them. You can get a longer list of possible places to speak in the free stuff section of my website. I keep adding more and more to the list all of the time.

Some students say, "Massive visibility? I could never do that. I'm too scared." I'm here to tell you that you can do it. All it takes is a conscious decision to overcome your fear and persistence.

Networking and charity groups: Attend networking groups and join charity groups that support your target market. If they have monthly meetings, become an officer so you can sit up front, appear as an authority, and be visible. If you can't become an officer, move to another group.

Toastmasters: All Toastmasters groups are run pretty much the same, but they all have different cultures. It you want to sell to corporate, join a corporate Toastmasters club. If you want to sell to entrepreneurs, or the general public, stay away from corporate groups.

Every group is a wonderful, accepting place that teaches the how tos of developing, formulating, and delivering top-notch speeches. They have lots of supportive members who are learning with you. Try a few groups before choosing one to join. They are very inexpensive and worth every penny. If you're afraid of speaking, these meetings are your new best friends and your next steps into the world of visibility.

Make sure to talk to the membership chair about the club's demographics before joining. Find a group with at least twenty-five members. Not everyone shows up every week. At these meetings, Toastmaster members are a captive audience. I used to get a lot of sales from my Toastmaster constituents. Why? Because I got to talk about what I do, try out my words and phrases, and receive instant feedback. Pretty cool, right?

Visit www.ToastmastersInternational.org to find a group near you.

Meetup Groups: Look for groups online. Type in your zip code and you'll get all of the groups in your local area. Again, choose only those in your target market. Your goal is to become visible and use your 3 Step Sales Waltz™.

Be consistent about attending the group events, and make an effort to get to know the members while building friendships. People must know, like, and trust you before working with you. You'll get business from members in the groups if you choose correctly and practice the 3 Step Sales Waltz™. I rarely walk out the door without finding a new client who is looking for the benefits I provide.

SPEAKING ON STAGE

Look online for speaking opportunities on stages, but be careful about what you agree to. There are many different formats, and most of them make you pay to stand there.

Here's how it works: A meeting planner gets a room. Then speakers flock to be on the stage to give a fifteen- or twenty-minute prepared speech. The exchange for speaking on stage is selling twelve $45 tickets to friends, associates, and family members interested in attending a networking event. This strategy provides $540 from each speaker. If the meeting planner has seven speakers, he make $3,780, which pays for the room and the lunch. If you don't sell all of your tickets, you are still required to pay for the tickets you didn't sell.

Some meeting planners include expert panels consisting of five speakers sitting on stage for twenty-five minutes, sharing their expertise for five minutes each. The panelists may be charged $450 each. If you're lucky, the meeting planner might throw in a year's membership to his community. This isn't always the best option because if you break this down, you'll find that you're paying $90 per minute to speak. This is great for the meeting planner, but it may not be so good for you. You can't have much influence in five minutes of speaking. Don't become a panelist unless you get a minimum of ten minutes, but you'll need to be wisely prepared to deliver a succinct, impactful message.

Other meeting planners may charge you a flat fee to speak or split your profits and sales 50 percent. Usually, it's better to pay the fee if you're confident you'll generate lots of sales.

Some membership groups charge an annual fee to join plus a small monthly fee. Don't be afraid to step up, but do your homework first. Ask whether others in the group are getting the benefits you desire.

During your speech, settle into your heart and wrap it around your most vulnerable story. Some coaches teach everyone the same techniques so you can almost identify the speaker's coach because it's so cookie cutter. Be your own person. What's used most frequently is to talk about what your life looks like today and then say, "But it wasn't always that way," and then run on with all of your hardships.

Do your best to be *you* authentically. Do not buy into the cookie-cutter clutter on stage. It's boring and unoriginal. Students who are taught the cookie-cutter technique are in classes with hundreds of others and aren't given the special attention necessary to step up authentically. If you've hired a cookie-cutter speaking coach, step away from the hordes of others and find another coach. It will make a world of difference in your income.

Dr. John Demartini says he rarely talks about the topic given to him because it's not always congruent with his audience's needs. He'll wrap the title into the speech, but then he'll read the audience members for their needs and provide what they are looking for.

There's no doubt, you are well aware of the information you want to provide on your topic. This allows you to deliver in a way that coincides with what the audience needs.

I attend many events and listen to speakers giving the same speech over and over again, and I can't begin to tell you how boring that is. A scripted speech is not the real authentic you. Carry an outline in your mind as you walk up the steps, and then deliver pieces of it based on how you read your audience. It will make a world of difference in your credibility and your sales from the stage.

STEPPING ONTO THE STAGE

Thirty minutes before stepping on stage, find a quiet place to reflect on your audience. Breathe deeply into your belly and focus on who your audience is, along with the needs and takeaways that will serve it best. Get out of your head and think, *What is the best message I can give my audience in this moment?* This takes the focus away from you, alleviates fear, and puts you in a heart-centered space while providing the information your people are looking for.

When you are called onto stage, engage and speak from your heart so you sound authentic from the moment you speak your very first words. Stay in your heart and speak to the audience members like they're all your best friends.

Always ask the meeting planner whether you can make an offer from the stage. If you can't make an offer, ask whether you can pass around a clipboard to get the names, phone numbers, and email addresses of people who might be interested in what you offer. In all cases, do not go sales-y while speaking on stage. If you can't do the clipboard, ask whether you can collect business cards. As a last resort, you can always tell people to go to the back of the room during the break and that you'll be waiting for them there.

If you are allowed to make an offer, be very careful not to be sales-y. Practice while watching your body language in the mirror, and do not step back under any circumstances. Stand squarely with feet shoulder-length apart. Engage and talk about the benefits you offer. If you step back, you will be perceived as insecure.

Many techniques work for making offers. To find the best ones for you, there are many videos on YouTube, and a multitude of speaking coaches available. In any case, before you spend the money to stand on stage and make an offer, practice your technique. It's too costly to practice on stage in front of others.

IMPLEMENTING YOUR PROFESSIONAL VIDEO CAMPAIGN

I prefer to speak my piece on video because no one else is vying for attention at the same time. Video tends to hold a person's undivided attention if the video is short and offers value to its recipients—the people in your database.

I have personally invited everyone in my database. I know who they are as people, and I do my best to provide value in business, finance, and sales through my Two-Minute Weekly Tips. If you'd like to receive my tips, you're welcome to sign up on my website at ShirleneReeves.com.

Providing value for your clients is rare in the media-marketing world, and most people are very busy, so they don't want to waste their time watching information that won't support them with the benefits they need. This is why it's so important to be aware of the benefits your clients want and are looking for before creating your videos.

An entrepreneur's favorite phrase around video production is, "Getting videos done is too expensive. Besides, I don't know how to show up or what to say." What if you knew how to show up professionally, were confident about what to say, and could produce your own videos from home? I do all of my videos for free, and so do my students.

Producing and editing your own videos isn't difficult when you know how to set up an inexpensive studio at home, complete with lighting, step and repeat banner, and video camera. After you've completed the exercise that educates you on what your clients are waiting to hear, you're on your way to making two-minute weekly videos you can send to your database for weekly top-of-awareness video marketing and blogs.

Keep in mind that it's not about how many people are receiving your videos; it's about the quality of the people who are interested in what you have to share. Remember to be respectful and don't barrage them with a bunch of advertising. Some people send out nothing but advertising, so you don't hear from them unless they're selling something.

I suggest that you build a relationship with your database community so they know and understand what you do. Offering them something for free and offering a program in the same email is the old conventional way of selling. Building relationships and giving from your heart makes it easier when it's time to offer a program they might benefit from and be interested in purchasing. It's best to send out three two-minute video tips and then a sales tip. You can always direct people back to your website if they want to take a second look into what you do. You never know when someone will need a benefit you provide, and they need to know where to look when they're ready. The wonderful friends in your database will willingly sign up for your list, and you'll find that more and more people will click through and watch your videos because they know you personally.

In the next segment, you'll discover how to maximize your income, find areas in your life where you can save money, and learn the Five Steps to Financial Freedom. Now that you know how to generate an income, it's time to take a look at how to keep your hard-earned money.

PART FOUR
MAXIMIZING YOUR WEALTH

"You are your greatest asset. Put your time, effort and money into training, grooming, and encouraging your greatest asset."

— Tom Hopkins

♡

CHAPTER 22

Discovering the Five Steps to Financial Freedom

As an entrepreneur, you might be reading this thinking that you don't make enough money at this time even to consider making financial decisions, but if you follow the blueprint I've provided for you, money is on your horizon, so you're going to need to know what to do with it to keep it safe.

Wouldn't it be awesome if you could make your money work for you rather than you working for your money for the rest of your life? That's what we're going to talk about in this segment of the book. You are going to learn how to make your money work for you instead of putting it in places that rob you of your hard-earned savings.

My personal mission is to educate you on how to protect yourself from the continued volatility in the markets, outshine minimal interest rates paid at the banks, overcome pension losses with tax-free retirement payments, provide accounts that secure your principle and actually grow without losses, and provide tips for how to live at home comfortably for the rest of your life. I know what you're thinking, and no, it's not too good to be true.

As a CFE Certified Financial Educator®, my goal is to support you in making money and saving the money you make. Specific steps are required for each path to accomplish your goals and dreams. It's really not hard to build wealth and protect it. All you need are the steps, practice, and the discipline to reach your desired goals.

It's possible that if you already have a financial advisor or financial planner, you're saying, "I'm taken care of. I don't need any more help." If this is true, that person must have taught you the simple, easy-to-understand financial principles that support you in making your own decisions, or did your financial advisor simply suggest an idea, give you a great reason for his suggestion, and you agreed with what he told you without doing any research on your own? I bet if I asked you right now what you are making in your IRA or 401k, you couldn't tell me. Time and again, I hear, "They told me, but I really didn't get it."

We all need to know and understand how to grow wealth and keep it. After all, how do we know where we're going if we don't have a map and a goal to get there? Sound familiar? I said that same thing about developing a viable, income-generating business, and it made sense, didn't it? Now we'll do it with a plan for your money.

DEFINING THE MEANING OF FINANCIAL FREEDOM

Everyone wants financial freedom, but what does that really mean? Some may say it's hard to define because it means something different to each person, and in some ways, that's true.

Financial freedom to me means I have the ability to enjoy my life, travel, spend time with family, drive a nice car, and have enough money to experience the finer things in life. Spend a moment to write down what financial freedom means to you.

I find it interesting that what we do for a living supports us in earning money, but we don't know what to do with the money once we have it. Most of us are only aware of how our parents handled debt and saved their money, but we have no idea how much debt or savings they were working with, so it was impossible to grasp firmly what we are supposed to do to live comfortably ourselves.

Building wealth and living financially free are frequently marketed and sold as materialistic experiences centered around the car you drive, the house you live in, designer clothing, and the jewelry you wear. These symbols are designed to make you appear successful, but in many cases, those who have these items are anything but financially free. In order to become the illusion those material items are creating, these people may be under mounds of credit card debt and pressured into singing, "I owe, I owe, so off to work I go," while they wave good-bye to their families and fight the traffic for hours.

These people haven't yet realized that for every dollar they spend, they need to put in more time at work to pay for the luxuries they possess. This is called trading time for money. Unfortunately, the majority of our population still lives paycheck to paycheck. We work all of our lives to have the *stuff*, and the stuff is what creates the monopoly of time at work that cripples our lifestyle. It's a vicious circle of hard work and feeling that we deserve more stuff because we worked so hard.

Here's the secret: Owning and paying for stuff is not a lifestyle. A lifestyle is living comfortably, with money coming in every month while you sleep. A lifestyle means you don't have to work so hard for your money because your money works for you, so you can have peace and time to relax on the beach.

Here's another secret: No one wants your stuff when you go. When my grandfather passed and I was left to clean out all of the stuff my grandparents had acquired over their lifetimes, it became painfully evident to me that we work all of our lives to buy what we think are treasures, when in reality, they only have meaning to you, and the kids are left with the decisions of how to get rid of them. Imagine how little we would need to work if we weren't addicted to buying the stuff.

Since this epiphany, I've felt a huge sense of freedom when walking into a store because I'm not attracted to the stuff. I focus on getting what I need and then leave, thereby saving thousands of dollars every year by not getting hooked into bright shiny objects and media advertising. As a result, I'm able to travel and live the lifestyle I deserve.

Simply wanting to retire or save for your kids' college plan isn't enough. Nobody cares as much about you and your family as you do, so wouldn't it be great to know when you can stop working and begin to enjoy a life of freedom you can spend with the people you love? I know of people who hate their jobs, but the money is so good that they won't quit, leaving them to live a life of pain. I'm just saying that it's a good idea to keep your mind open and wake up to new, more effective lifestyle ideas that can support you in reaching financial freedom and security.

THE FIVE STEPS TO FINANCIAL FREEDOM

To achieve financial freedom, you need to take five steps. We'll look at each of these steps in detail in the pages that follow:

1. Create Cash Flow
2. Ensure Proper Protection
3. Manage Debt
4. Maintain an Emergency Fund
5. Save Long-Term

Step 1: Create Cash Flow—for when there's a little too much month left at the end of your money.

Having a strong and steady cash flow is the beginning of great success. It seems like a long uphill climb, especially if you don't have the cash flow to keep a roof over your head and food on your table. Your cash flow must be positive or everything in your universe stops except for the bills that continue to tumble onto your kitchen table relentlessly every month.

As business owners or solopreneurs, we often pay for branding, building websites, and marketing, believing that the dollars will soon begin to flow in and once again fill our coffers. Then, we look at our bank accounts and all of our savings have disappeared. "How did that happen?" we think as a shot of fear instantly grips our gut and we begin to panic. Believe me; you're not alone. I hear this from entrepreneurs almost daily.

Coaches who tell you not to get a job are detrimental to your health. Living in your car or couch-surfing isn't the answer. Find a job right now, any job. Don't worry about what it is. Just get something, and get some cash flowing in. Remember, this job is only temporary so you can once again take the steps toward financial freedom.

Step 2: Ensure Proper Protection

Will Rogers made a good point for all of us to consider when he said, "The man who dies without adequate life insurance should have to come back and see the mess he's created."

Proper Protection means making sure you are insured to protect your cash flow, your home, your hard-earned savings, and your family's future. This may mean: car insurance, health insurance, long-term care, disability, and life insurance.

Quietly reflect on what your family members would do if you were no longer there to support them? Is there enough money in your emergency fund and financial reserves for them to continue living comfortably? Would your family members be forced to uproot themselves, leave their home, and move at their most grief-stricken time of life? Will your children still be able to go to college, or will they be required to give up their dreams and go to work to support the family? The biggest question is: Would you be putting the family you cherish in peril if something happened to you?

Life insurance as an investment policy

Think of your life insurance as an investment in your family's future. Some say they know they need life insurance, but they don't want another monthly payment. But they don't understand that this payment is not an expense or a liability. Your home mortgage payments and car payments are liabilities because those are paid month after month. Life insurance is considered to be a living asset.

Did you know that life insurance has been around since the days of ancient Rome? Caius Marius, a Roman military leader, created a burial club among his troops, so in the event of the unexpected death of a club member, other members would pay for the funeral expenses.

Think Advisor wrote on the web that:

> The Romans believed anyone who was improperly buried would become an unhappy ghost, so the clubs were embraced by the government and military because of the deep conviction that it was absolutely essential for each person, regardless of social standing, to be buried in the correct manner. The clubs later evolved to also provide a stipend to the survivors of the deceased.

We definitely don't want any unhappy ghosts around, but there are seven more pertinent reasons life insurance is important. Often, my clients aren't clear about the differences in the types of life insurance and how they might relate to their lives. Some even say, "Why do I need it?"

Unfortunately, most people don't buy it; it is sold to them and they wind up wondering whether it's something they really need. While it may seem like the latter is true, there are seven reasons why I believe you should purchase life insurance:

1. **To Pay Final Expenses:** Funeral and burial costs can easily run into the tens of thousands of dollars. This expense can be overwhelming to the spouse, the parents, or the children who can no longer attend college. Dealing with a challenge such as this during the grieving period causes unnecessary emotional and financial fears and suffering.

2. **To Cover Children's Expenses:** If you have children, you want to be sure your kids are well taken care of and can be provided a quality college education. For this reason, additional coverage is absolutely essential while the kids are still living at home.

3. **To Replace the Spouse's Income:** If your spouse passes away, while the kids are young, replacing your spouse's income is

essential to maintaining your lifestyle. You may need to hire help with the kids so you can continue working to support your family

4. **To Pay Off Debt:** In addition to providing income to cover everyday living expenses, you will still need to cover your debt, and insurance can help. When you receive the life insurance check, the money can be utilized to cover credit card debts or pay off the mortgage so you won't have to sell the house. Can you imagine how difficult it would be to pack up everything you own and move the kids to another school because you can't afford to stay where you are?

5. **To Buy a Business Partner's Shares:** If you or your spouse is in a business partnership, you'll want to make sure you and your partner have key-man insurance. Then if one of you dies, the surviving partner will have enough cash to buy his interest from the heirs and cover the company's obligations without having to sell the company itself. Either surviving partner will have the same needs (due to the risk that one might die), and each should simultaneously purchase insurance on the other's life.

6. **To Pay Off Estate Taxes:** Estate taxes can be astronomical, so having insurance in place to pay them is important to avoid jeopardizing assets or funds built for retirement. Use of insurance for this purpose is most common in large estates, and uses permanent (rather than term) insurance to ensure that coverage remains until the end of life.

7. **Financial Tax Planning:** Life insurance offers you the ability to transfer a policy's death benefit income-tax-free to beneficiaries. No matter how big the life insurance payment is, your beneficiaries won't pay a single cent of income tax on the money they get. What other investment does that?

How Much Life Insurance Do I Need?

The amount of life insurance you should purchase varies, but you can easily figure it out by adding your total debt, including your mortgage, four years of college tuition per child, and burial expenses. Once you know this number, you can then take the steps necessary to decide which policy best suits your current lifestyle, knowing that it can be reduced at a later date if you choose a Universal Life Insurance policy.

Total debt (including credit cards and car payments):_____

Mortgage balance or rent for 12 months: _____

College tuition annually per child times 4 years: _____

Any additional loans: _____

Burial expenses: _____

Total of how much life insurance you need _____

Types of Insurance Policies

Insurance policies vary so it's prudent that you choose a policy that fits your lifestyle. Review the types of life insurance available. You've already learned the uses and the purpose of choosing life insurance and figured your total insurance need, so now it's time to choose the type of policy you desire.

> **Term Life:** The first form is one of pure protection—the Term Plan is usually in force for periods from ten to thirty years—when you need a large face value for a limited time

period. This policy pays only on the death of the policy-holder. It is pure insurance and has the lowest premium for the highest payout. If you survive the term of the policy, you do not receive any payment. Your premiums only go toward insuring your life. There is no investment made out of your premiums in a Term Plan.

When the insurance term comes to an end, it can be extremely expensive. Some clients have two or three term policies. They ride out the policies to the end of their term and then decide they want a permanent type of insurance (Whole Life or Universal Life) that totals the same amount as the term insurance policies offer. But these people are now older, and sometimes unhealthy, so the cost of getting insurance in the same amount becomes extremely expensive and is frequently prohibitive. It's better to get a permanent type of insurance at a younger age because the monthly payments stay the same.

Whole Life: A permanent policy that is designed to stay in force until you die. As long as you purchase one with a "level" premium and a level face value, neither the premium nor the benefit will change. You will always pay the same premium from the day you make the purchase until the day you die. Traditional whole life insurance, also known as ordinary life or straight life, is a type of permanent (cash value) insurance that provides coverage for your entire life.

If you withdraw cash from a cash value life insurance policy, the amount of withdrawals up to your basis in the policy will be tax-free. Generally, your basis is the amount of premiums you have paid into the policy less any dividends or withdrawals you have previously taken.

Universal Life (UL): Universal Life is intended to combine permanent insurance coverage with greater flexibility in premium payments, along with the potential for greater growth of cash values. This policy arrived after the Whole Life policy with an added savings benefit. The excess of premium payments above the current cost of insurance is credited monthly to the cash value of the policy with interest, as well as any other policy charges and fees drawn from the cash value, even if no premium payment is made that month. Interest credited to the account is determined by the insurer, but it has a contractual minimum rate (often 2 percent).

Universal Life insurance addresses the perceived disadvantages of Whole Life—namely that premiums and death benefits are fixed. With Universal Life, both the premiums and death benefit are flexible, meaning that they can be either increased or decreased depending on the owner's needs. In other words, an owner may want higher insurance while the children are still living at home and later choose to decrease the insurance when the children are on their own and the mortgage is paid down.

Indexed Universal Life: When an earnings rate is pegged to a financial index such as stocks, bonds, or another interest rate index, the Universal Life insurance policy is considered to be an "Indexed Universal Life" contract. These types of policies offer the advantage of guaranteed level premiums throughout the insured's lifetime, at a substantially lower premium cost than an equivalent Whole Life policy at first; the cost of insurance is always increasing, as you grow older. Your payments stay the same, but as you age, the monthly cost increases and the payment difference is paid out of the savings feature.

There are many hybrids offered in the industry that provide different options called living benefits. They are all priced differently and offer different options, but there are a number of things to keep in mind while deciding which policy to choose:

> **Long-Term Care or Critical Care Policy Rider:** When you wrap one of these options into a policy, you are not throwing your money away on a stand-alone long-term care policy if you want long-term or critical care, but don't elect or need to use it. Tips: 1) Choose a policy that pays outside of the United States if you intend to move to a place other than the United States. 2) Most policies request receipts for reimbursement of long-term or critical care. Choose a policy that pays a monthly check without receipts so you can use the money without paying someone to collect, define, and enter the monthly costs. This can get very expensive and eat into your reimbursements.

> **Tax-Free Withdrawals:** In some policies, you can withdraw an income from your policy, after ten years, tax-free and not be required to pay it back. The idea is that the policy grows as you make your monthly payments over a long period of time, and then you can withdraw the money (loan it to yourself) to use for college tuition, buying a house, travel, and supplementing your income. Understand that there are withdrawal amount limitations, so read your brochure carefully when planning on which policy to purchase.

When you decide on which insurance policy works best for you, stick with it. Closing and taking the money out of a long-term policy can be very expensive, and you may trigger a taxable event with surprise consequences. Check with your accountant prior to closing any life insurance policy. Insurance policies are meant to be a part of your overall tax and financial planning benefits.

Finding the Money for Proper Protection

Did you know that if you save just $10 a day, you will have $300 a month to put toward life insurance and build cash value within your policy? If you don't know where to find $300, look at the "Uncovering Unnecessary Expenses" section, and I'm sure you'll find the money you need to provide for your family.

If you make over $100,000 per year, you can apply for a life insurance policy with bank payment assistance at no cost to you. It's amazing how it works, so if the payment is the problem, you might want to consider looking into this. *But I have bad credit!* you might be thinking. Credit is not an issue because there's only a medical qualification.

You can find $10 a day by saving on Starbucks lattes, partying, video games, fancy toys, big-screen TVs, and eating out. This is also a great way to save consistently toward your tax-free retirement. So many say, "I can't save because I don't make enough money." Are you sure that's absolutely true? You haven't yet looked at how you're spending the money you're making.

With discipline and a strategy, saving is definitely doable and can be tailored specifically to meet your needs and those of your family. If you need money for your child's college tuition, emergencies, beginning a new business, or anything else you deem necessary, you could borrow some of the cash value in some life insurance policies, after three years, provided you have deposited enough to borrow. After ten years, you can borrow the money, interest-free and tax-free, from some policies, and never be required to pay the money back.

A New Path to Cash

Have you thought about saving your money in a secure Universal Life Insurance Policy? This policy outperformed other investments during our most difficult last ten years. You will never feel the losses or the volatility in the markets while enjoying growth in this hybrid.

Do you have a business partner? If you're an entrepreneur in a partnership, think carefully about insuring each partner to protect the other from heirs who may lay claim to half of your company if your partner dies.

If you have key man insurance, the heirs will be paid, and you can hire someone to replace your partner's talents immediately, thereby insuring that your company continues to run smoothly and the heirs walk away satisfied.

Where Are You Saving Today?

If your money is in a 401k, SEP, IRA, or 203b, you cannot borrow from your account until you're 59½ without paying penalties and taxes. These are what the IRS calls "qualified funds." Prior to that age, you'll pay taxes and penalties if you borrow the money and aren't able to put the money back into your account after a specific period of time. Check with your accountant if you feel you need to take this step. It's very risky.

At 59½, you will owe taxes on the money you draw out for both the state and the feds, but you will not pay penalties. At 70½, you are required to take a minimum percentage of your total overall account each year, or pay penalties. Any monies you draw out of your qualified account are taxable in that year.

Again, I suggest you consult your accountant for overall tax planning. It's a good policy to maintain a relationship with your accountant and ask what the consequences are prior to acting on decisions that may cause unplanned or unintentional taxable events.

Step 3: Managing Debt

Many small monthly payments, rolled together, become an avalanche of debt that depletes your monthly cash flow. I know a woman I'll call Maggie who lives on Maui. She has an amazing life of walking the beach in the morning, swimming in the ocean on late afternoons, and watching beautiful ocean sunsets from her deck.

"What does she do the rest of her day?" you might ask. She has a habit of sitting in front of the TV watching the home shopping networks, purchasing what she believes are great buys, and committing to "flex-payments"—three months for this payment and four months for another—ramping up ongoing debt. It makes her husband crazy.

It seems that my Maui acquaintance has more than one type of problem, but it's obvious that she doesn't understand the conspiracy behind how the home shopping networks reach into our pockets. These shows specialize in pushing tons of products for small monthly payments, which they finance over months at a time, while digging deeper and deeper into your savings account. Talk about an amazing sales technique.

These programs all have "flex pay," and if you don't keep an accounting of how much is added to your total monthly expenses, they will drive you under financially. They make the payments so small that their loyal customers think, "That's really cheap. I can afford that," while reaching for the phone to place the another order financed on plastic.

Maggie was a retired airline stewardess who finds this way of shopping very enticing. She loves not having to drive to the store, walk around the mall, or carry anything home. All she had to do is make the call and provide her credit card number before the countdown clock expires. After five years of this behavior, Maggie has amassed a whole room of unopened boxes all full of brand new items purchased from the home shopping networks.

At first, Maggie's husband, Randy, wasn't aware of her habit. He was an electrician who contributed a great deal of income to the household as an independent contractor. Over the months, I watched as he became aware of the situation and then more and more despondent over the ever-increasing debt. Even though he spoke to Maggie about it, he couldn't seem to get through to her enough to make it stop. He didn't realize he was dealing with an addiction or he may have taken additional steps to resolve the problem.

Together, with Maggie's retirement checks and Randy's income, they were able to manage the astronomical credit card debt until Randy fell off a ladder at work and broke his heel. For two years, Randy wasn't able to work and had no disability. They were left with only Maggie's retirement income and their savings to meet their creditors' demands. In 2008, the debt washed over them and everything Randy had worked for his entire life vanished almost immediately, including his presence here on earth.

The following Easter, Randy committed suicide. Maggie is now couch-surfing among the few friends she still has left. However, her mountain of debt still looms while her "stuff" resides in thrift shops all over the island. It's a sad story, but certainly one to keep in mind. What do your monthly payments add up to?

Uncovering Unnecessary Expenses

You might think you know how much you spend daily, but I feel confident in saying that you probably don't. In this day and age, it's so easy to spend money without thinking about it. We almost never carry cash, so we have no concept of the total amount of money we are spending unless we run out before the bills are paid.

I suggest you make a note of every dollar you spend for one week. I did this recently and found that I was spending an average of $100 a day. I had no idea I was gobbling up $3,000 a month on top of the money already budgeted to pay my bills.

Here's what I found…

Starbucks: $31.50 a week; $126 a month; $1,512 a year; $7,560 in five years.

Daily trips to the coffee shop to pay for a yummy shot of caffeine. It was actually an addiction that I later noticed was calling me in every time I drove by a green Starbucks awning. If you enjoy Starbucks, stop going there and find out how it calls you into the store. It's a great gimmick. The company makes millions on it. How much does your addiction cost you?

Audible: $26 a month or $312 per year = $1,560 for five years

Audible makes it easy to buy books, and the company sells its service by telling us we can buy books with credits and get them cheaper than the original book price. These company memberships are like blood-lines to their company bank accounts that they budget on automatically coming in every month.

Facial Cream Product: $90 a month or $1,080 per year = $5,400 for five years.

Many times, we request something for free, off the Internet, and forget to cancel it. Then you begin receiving the product monthly and it dings your bank account before you even notice. You may think, like I did once, "This is a great product. I guess I'll keep it." Then when I calculated the cost, it was easy to say no, but a real pain to stop the next shipment and go to the post office to return the product just received.

TV package: $120 a month or $1,440 per year = $7,200 for five years

Internet: $89 a month or $1,068 per year = $5,400 for five years

I live in San Diego where we are limited to either Time Warner or Comcast. Since Time Warner has the highest Internet speed for my live streaming and class trainings, there isn't much choice. I run my two-day intensive courses on Zoom and create videos on Google Hangout, so I have a connection of 100 mbps. I'm forced to stick with this program, but if I find a way to reduce the costs, I'll jump into action.

Vitamin Supplements: $90 a month or $1,080 per year = $5,400 for five years.

Eating Out: $300 a month or $3,600 per year = $18,000 for five years.

With an alcoholic beverage: monthly cost is $384 per month or $6,528 per year = $24,960 for five years.

In the calculations above, I'm figuring $25 per meal for only three meals out per week. Of course, this doesn't include $120 a month in groceries and no alcohol. If you add wine or alcohol, there will be an additional $7 to $10 per glass per meal.

Calculating additional monthly expenses

Expense	Weekly	Monthly	Annually	Five Years
Starbucks	31.50	126.00	1,512.00	7,560.00
Audible	6.50	26.00	312.00	1,560.00
Facial Cream	22.50	90.00	1,080.00	5,400.00
TV Package	30.00	120.00	1,440.00	7,200.00
Internet	22.25	89.00	1,068.00	5,340.00
Vitamins	22.50	90.00	1,080.00	5,400.00
Eating Out	75.00	300.00	3,600.00	18,000.00
TOTALS	**$210.25**	**$841.00**	**$10,092.00**	**$50,460.00**

Adjusting the monthlies by reducing, replacing, or eliminating expenses.

Below, be sure to note the last column in this chart indicating the total savings of $29,831 over a five-year period.

Expense	Weekly	Monthly	Annually	5 Year SAVINGS
Starbucks	3.33	15.00	180.00	6,660.00
Audible	Cancelled			1,560.00
Facial Cream	Cancelled			5,400.00
Netflix	2.00	7.99	95.88	6,721.00
Internet	22.25	89.00	1,068.00	0
Vitamins	22.50	90.00	1080.00	0
Eating Out	16.25	32.50	1,690	9,550.00
TOTALS	**$56.33**	**$225.32**	**$2,703**	**Saved $29,831.00**

I cut the TV off completely and switched to Netflix at $7.99 a month. They have all the programming I need, and I am no longer subject to commercials and the opinions of news stations.

I rarely eat out and focus on preparing and eating nutritious foods at home or with friends. $267.50 per month saved.

The facial cream: Cancelled and returned for a credit.

Audible would not return my money, but it stopped the monthly charge and is allowing me to purchase books for the balance on my account of $225. That's a lot of books that I don't need, but I'm stuck with it.

I only go to Starbucks when I'm traveling or when meeting with a client. I add $50 refills to my Starbucks card, which makes it easy to keep track of how much I'm spending. Each time I add money to the card, Starbucks gives me a free drink and I write the whole thing off because I use it for business. This strategy has cut my Starbucks costs down to about $15 a month.

Thinking It Over

Do your numbers. Keep track of what you spend per week, and then look at what you are obligated to pay on a monthly basis. Think about it. If you weren't wasting so much money, you wouldn't have to work so hard.

All of these companies are living off of your hard-earned dollars. Keep in mind that what I've shared with you are my personal expenses. These figures don't include credit card interest because I don't have any credit card debt. If you pay monthly interest on your cards, include those costs.

Asking Yourself Tell-Tale Questions

- Do you drink sodas and expensive energy drinks?
- Do you smoke? That will be a painful number both for your health and your bank account.
- Do you drive an expensive car that could be exchanged for something cheaper but still nice?
- Have you checked on auto insurance to see whether you can get a less expensive rate?
- Have you refinanced your car to the lowest interest rate?
- Are you paying a mortgage for a big home with rooms you don't use? Rent them out on Air B&B to supplement your mortgage payments.
- Are you drinking your profits? Alcohol is both expensive and addictive. Take stock of how much you spend on alcohol.

The whole idea is to get your money flowing in and minimize the money you spend. Did you know that the average American's income is approximately $30,000 a year? Why not think more in terms of investments than consumption. If you're spending every dime and not carefully watching how your money is spent, it will be impossible to invest in your future. By the way, your 401k or SEP IRA is not an investment. We'll talk more about this later.

Paying with Plastic is Like Playing with Fire

In my first year of college, I experienced a scary financial burden, and it was all Visa's fault. Just kidding. I was only eighteen when my first Visa card arrived in the mail with my name on it. That was pretty exciting, and like many young people today, that little plastic card gave me license to "Have a blast!"

Talk about a rude awakening. Looking back now, I'm glad I learned my credit card lesson at an early age. The pain of the monthly payments created a lifetime reminder that I'll never repeat. In only thirty days, I was suddenly responsible for $1,200 in debt, so I needed to devise a way to pay it off, while I was collecting only one small part-time paycheck and going to college. In the next segment, I share what I know works.

Getting Rid of Debt to Dig Your Way Out

Set up four columns. Label them "Credit Card," "Total Debt," "Monthly Payment," and "Interest Rate." Organize the credit card list beginning with the card that has the highest interest rate first.

With this list, you can easily determine the following:

1. Your total debt: At this point, there is no need to be concerned about this number. It is what it is, and it's done unless there are purchases you can return for credit.

2. Determine which card is costing you the greatest amount of interest and is the most expensive to maintain.

3. Note how much it costs to pay the monthly minimum payments on each card.

Your goal is to pay off one card at a time while making minimum payments on the others. Begin focusing on the card with the highest interest rate, but if you find there's another card with minimal debt, choose that one first so you can pay it off in a shorter period of time and eliminate it. When I say eliminate, I mean cut it up and celebrate.

It's important to stay focused on paying off the first card and doing what you can to eliminate any further charges on any of the cards. As you write the check or pay online, say out loud, "I am paying off all debt." This will support you in manifesting the payoff much more quickly.

Each month, pay an extra $25 or more from the money you've saved in the daily spending exercise you just completed. If you were able to save more, then pay more or pay an additional $25 twice a month.

After paying off the first card, move to the next one. When paying this payment, add the minimum statement payment required, plus an extra $25, plus the full payment you put toward the first card. You are no longer paying on the first card so there will be extra money to put toward the second card until you pay that one off. Don't forget to cut the second card up and celebrate when you send the final payment. This is very important.

Next, you'll begin paying off the third card. With this card, you'll add $75 to the minimum payment so you can pay it off much faster. Continue to add $25 to each subsequent card, plus the total amount you paid on the last card, while remembering each time you make a payment to say, "I am paying off all debt." If you have a fourth card, you'll pay $100 plus the minimum payment and so on.

Important Audit Reminder: Once all the cards are paid off, select two cards to keep. One card is for business purposes, and the other card is for personal use. This is extremely important because if the IRS audits you for your business, you don't want them auditing your personal records and vice versa. Blending the two on one card is a nightmare for both you and your accountant if you land on the audit list. Remember this tip to protect yourself.

In the future, charge only what you are able to pay, in full, in that month. Never let a month go by without paying off your credit card(s) unless it's an emergency.

Step 4: Maintain an Emergency Fund

Maintaining an emergency fund can resolve expensive, inconvenient complications.

One of my assistants, Trish, was living check to check, and there wasn't much room in her bank account or her budget for unexpected surprises. One warm August morning, she walked into my office dripping in sweat and out of breath. "My car just died at the bottom of the hill," she said. "I have to rent a car until I can pay the ransom to get mine out of the shop. Now I have to pay the tow truck, the shop, plus daily storage costs until I can afford to get it fixed, the car rental, my car payment, and my insurance. Can somebody drive me over to rent a car?" Trish hadn't yet realized that she'd already lost more than half a day of pay. *How far can you stretch one check?* I wondered. Not to mention, she had made a big deal about all of the clothes she'd bought just the week before.

As a rule of thumb, employees should work toward saving an emergency fund with a minimum of six to twelve months of total household expenses. Entrepreneurs and independent contractors should save between twelve and eighteen months of household income for emergencies and times when work may be hard to find.

Is this impossible? No? You'll see that it's possible after you've paid off your credit cards and completed the "Monthly Expenses" exercise. If my assistant hadn't been spending money on clothing she didn't need, she could have put money in her emergency fund. Then only the costs of the repair and car rental would have been required, saving her thousands of dollars.

Step 5: Save Long-Term

This topic covers 401Ks, SEP IRAs, kids' college plans, mutual funds, stocks, bonds, and any type of account you are saving money in long-term, with the intention of using it for retirement or putting your child through college.

I often ask my clients, "How is your cash flow?" and they respond with, "I'm stuffing my 401k like crazy." Employees are led to believe that a 401k is their saving grace for retirement, when, in reality, it may not be the best route for reaching your retirement goals and living the lifestyle of your dreams. Unfortunately, that's not what your accountant would say.

I suggest that you don't put money in your 401k before paying off your debt, saving an emergency fund, or protecting your family. Definitely stop feeding your 401k if you don't have enough cash flow to feed your family.

Long-term saving is always the last step, not the first. Be careful not to invert your pyramid of five steps to financial freedom. Be sure to protect yourself and your cash flow first. In the next chapter, we'll be rethinking the challenges and volatility of what it means to maintain your money in the market without keeping a careful eye on it.

"Don't let the opinions of the average man sway you. Dream, and he thinks you're crazy. Succeed, and he thinks you're lucky. Acquire wealth, and he thinks you're greedy. Pay no attention. He simply doesn't understand."

— Robert G. Allen

♡

CHAPTER 23

Rethinking Market-Driven Investments and Long-Term Savings

One of the biggest problems I see today is that people put money into long-term savings before meeting and completing the first four steps. Putting money in accounts like this causes you to pay for your needs on credit cards with astronomical interest. It doesn't make sense to receive so little in the markets when you are required to pay so much interest on debt. Make sure you have enough cash flow to pay off your debt and secure your cash flow with proper protection. Then save an emergency fund so you won't be required to create astronomical surprise charges on your cards. Then and only then do you contribute to a 401k or Sep IRA, if you seriously believe you need to.

Below I've listed four reasons why you may want to reconsider investing in qualified funds accounts. Instead, I suggest you diversify and layer your financial strategy with both secure and volatile accounts, while electing to pay fewer taxes, alleviating losses, and in some accounts, grow your money tax-free.

There are four reasons why you may want to rethink your 401k or IRA account contributions. The media has been telling us, "It's time to retire your retirement account," and there are a number of pointers I'll give you for why, the primary one being: You have no control of your own money.

Each plan has an administrator and usually offers a variety of mutual fund packages. The purpose of investing in mutual funds is that it may be safer to invest in a variety of stocks instead of individual stocks with more volatility.

Before contributing, even if the company is offering a small matching percentage, ask yourself a few questions:

1. How much control do I have of my money once I make the contribution?
2. How much am I really saving in taxes if I pay the taxes now and contribute to an account that grows tax-free and protects my family?
3. If I put money in the 401k, will I have enough cash flow to pay my mortgage, put food on the table, and pay off my debt?
4. What happens when the market goes down? Do I lose my money?

Let's address each question one at a time.

1. How much control do I have of my money once I make the contribution?

Once you put your money in a qualified 401k or SEP IRA retirement account, you can't take it out without paying penalties and taxes, depending on the state you file your taxes in. When the market takes a dive like it did in 2007-2008, there is nothing you can do to save it but stand by, in shock, watching as it sinks to the bottom. You are completely at the mercy of the fund managers and the IRS. However, if you are fast, you could call the administrator and move the funds into a qualified savings account, but the fund managers will have to sell the mutual fund stocks off first. I learned this the hard way. When I tried to stop the downward slide, I wasn't able to sell off the mutual funds fast enough, and the fund manager took his fees on the way down, so I was left with nothing.

"But I made all my money back," you might say. Sure you did, but after ten years, it's only back to where it was when you started in 2007. You've lost ten years of growth so you'll have to work an additional ten years to make up for the losses the market created for you.

Never put your money in a place where you can't manage it. I love to ask my clients, "What's going on with your retirement money? What is it invested in, and how is it doing?" They are never able to tell me. Don't get caught putting your money in a 401K and then look the other way or there may not be any money there when you you look again.

"But my employer matches my donation at 3 percent. That's a good thing right?" Sure it is, but if the market gobbles it up, what's the point? Oh, and I didn't tell you the best part about these retirement accounts. There may be up to seventeen different fees per account. Even the media has been telling everyone to retire their retirement accounts. Maybe it's time to listen and make the change.

2. **What's the difference in taxes if I pay the taxes now and contribute to an account that grows tax-free and protects my family?**

According to the historical chart, taxes are the lowest they've been in seventy-two years. You can also see that they've been increasing since 2013. This is why it makes sense to pay the taxes now rather than defer them and tie your money up in a qualified account until the age of 59½. Since the tax brackets are still low and appear to be on the rise, doesn't it make more sense to pay your taxes now? Think about what you could do with your money if it wasn't in a place out of your reach. You could buy a house, pay for college, travel, and, of course, add to your emergency fund or pay off debt.

No one in the financial industry has a crystal ball, but you can pretty much depend on the government to raise the taxes. The government makes all of the decisions about the tax brackets and their increases. Those representatives we vote for are free to change the tax brackets whenever they decide money is needed to pay off debt, and we all are aware of the vast amount of debt the US government owes. This fact makes it difficult to plan for our future lifestyle. What if you begin drawing on your qualified funds and the taxes are at 50, 70, or 91 percent? What will your lifestyle look like when you're at an age when working is no longer an option? Wouldn't it be better to plan now, put your money into the safety of a guaranteed no loss account, and let it grow?

Take a look at the historical tax history chart below. It will give you an idea of how the tax rates fluctuate. If you wait and pay your taxes later, you may pay a much higher tax, which will be much more expensive. In other words, instead of paying a shrimp's worth of taxes now, you'll be subject to letting the government take the lobster in taxes later. You have a choice. Pay the shrimp now or the lobster later. It's entirely up to you.

Historical Highest Marginal Income Tax Rates

Top Marginal Rate		Top Marginal Rate		Top Marginal Rate	
Year	Rate	Year	Rate	Year	Rate
1913	7.0%	1948	82.13%	1983	50.00%

1914	7.0%	1949	82.13%	1984	50.00%
1915	7.0%	1950	84.36%	1985	50.00%
1916	15.0%	1951	91.00%	1986	50.00%
1917	67.0%	1952	92.00%	1987	39.50%
1918	77.0%	1953	92.00%	1988	28.00%
1919	73.0%	1954	91.00%	1989	28.00%
1920	73.0%	1955	91.00%	1990	28.00%
1921	73.0%	1956	91.00%	1991	31.00%
1922	58.0%	1957	91.00%	1992	31.00%
1923	43.5%	1958	91.00%	1993	39.60%
1924	46.0%	1959	91.00%	1994	39.60%
1925	25.0%	1960	91.00%	1995	39.60%
1926	25.0%	1961	91.00%	1996	39.60%
1927	25.0%	1962	91.00%	1997	39.60%
1928	25.0%	1963	91.00%	1998	39.60%
1929	24.0%	1964	77.00%	1999	39.60%
1930	25.0%	1965	70.00%	2000	39.60%
1931	25.0%	1966	70.00%	2001	39.10%
1932	63.0%	1967	70.00%	2002	38.60%
1933	63.0%	1978	75.25%	2003	35.00%
1934	63.0%	1969	77.00%	2004	35.00%
1935	63.0%	1970	71.75%	2005	35.00%
1936	79.0%	1971	70.00%	2006	35.00%
1937	79.0%	1972	70.00%	2007	35.00%
1938	79.0%	1973	70.00%	2008	35.00%
1939	79.0%	1974	70.00%	2009	35.00%
1940	81.10%	1975	70.00%	2010	35.00%
1941	81.00%	1976	70.00%	2011	35.00%
1942	88.00%	1977	70.00%	2012	35.00%
1943	88.00%	1978	70.00%	2013	39.60%
1944	94.00%	1979	70.00%	2014	39.60%

1945	94.00%	1980	70.00%	2015	39.60%
1946	86.45%	1981	69.13%	2016	39.60%
1947	86.45%	1982	50.00%	2017	39.60%

Note: This table contains a number of simplifications and ignores a number of factors, such as a maximum tax on earned income of 50 percent when the top rate was 70 percent and the current increase in rates due to income related reductions in value of itemized deductions. Perhaps, most importantly, it ignores the large increase in percentage of returns that were subject to this top rate.

Sources: Eugene Steuerle, The Urban Institute; Joseph Pechman, Federal Tax Policy; Joint Committee on Taxation, Summary of Conference Agreement on the Jobs and Growth Tax Relief Reconciliation Act of 2003, JCX-54-03, May 22, 2003; IRS Revenue Procedures, various years.

3. **If I put money in a 401k, will I have enough cash flow to pay my mortgage, put food on the table, and pay off debt?**

    Before contributing to a 401k, look at your net income after taxes, and determine how much income you'll have each month. Then add up your personal and business expenses so you'll know whether you can afford to contribute to your 401k or Sep IRA. If you only contribute to an IRA, you may have enough write-offs to offset your contribution or simply pay the shrimp in taxes.

4. **What happens when the market goes down? Do I lose my money?**

    Would you gamble your hard-earned retirement money? My guess is you would answer, "No!" You wouldn't dream of throwing your hard-earned money down on a crap-shoot. That would be crazy, wouldn't it? Well, guess what? You are gambling your money in a 401k or SEP IRA.

The market is unpredictable and volatile. Every time the points go down, so does your savings. You might say, "Yeah, but it goes back up again, and I'm in it for the long haul." If you're forty-five or older, your long haul is over. After all, how long do you want to work to make up for your losses in the market?

You may think that when the market goes down 100 points one day and back up 100 points the next, you still have the same amount of money you started with. Not so. Every time the market goes down, you lose money so you start at a lower amount of money when it goes back up. That's why we call it "eroding away at your bottom line." Each trip down sweeps a little more money out of your account. Each donation into your 401k may be a gift to the market.

If you're wondering where to put your money, after paying the taxes, I'd be happy to give you a free forty-minute consultation. During that time, we can talk specifically about your personal financial challenges and design a plan that is safe. I'll share about my favorite strategy in the next chapter. Pretty much everyone loves it.

Fixed annuities in today's investment products are a great tool for securing and growing your money. They aren't your grandpa's or Suze Orman's annuities anymore. Some offer great bonuses, depending on the plan you choose, and a much higher interest rate than you can get in a bank savings account.

Many Annuities provide a plan that pays you an income throughout your lifetime when you elect to take the rider. They are a safe investment for growing your money and could offer one of four streams of income during your retirement.

What if you could invest your money and it doubled in ten to twelve years? If you want to save and grow money that is other than qualified funds, meaning you've already paid the taxes on the principle, you will only be required to pay taxes on the earnings in small amounts when you receive the payments.

Rolling Over Right

If you were laid off or left a job and paid into a retirement account, it is best not to roll the money into the next hiring company. Take this opportunity to put the money in a safe place where it will grow so you don't lose it in the market. Keep in mind that the 401k funds are considered to be qualified funds that you can roll into an IRA account. Always keep your qualified funds in a qualified account. If the mistake of rolling your money into a non-qualified account occurs, you will be required to pay taxes on all of the money in the same tax year the incident occurred.

When you file your taxes, after rolling your money into a qualified account, you will be sent a statement. Give the statement to your accountant when you file your taxes or it will be assumed by the IRS that you took the money out of the qualified account and a taxable event will be triggered. This can easily be resolved by requesting a statement from the insurance company that maintains your rollover account.

Where can I grow my money safely? you might be thinking. Now is a good time to talk about annuities, the protection they provide, and their differences so you can make an informed decision.

What Is an Annuity?

An annuity is a contract with an insurance company. Annuities all have one feature in common that makes them very different from other financial products. The insurance company promises to pay you an income regularly for a specific period of time, based on the choices you make, including for the rest of your life.

Some are called immediate annuities because they begin paying you an income right after you buy them. Others are deferred annuities that begin paying at a later date. The most common annuities used are deferred annuities, so let's look more closely into how they are alike and different so you can make an educated decision about what you want to do with your IRA or 401k roll-over before speaking with me or your financial advisor. Retired investors like this strategy because they can keep their money safe, grow it, and elect to receive a lifetime income from that money to live on.

How Deferred Annuities Are Similar

- All deferred annuities have an accumulation period and a specific payout period. Different annuities accumulate money in different ways, and the value of your annuity changes based on the type of annuity you choose. During the payout period, the insurance company will make income payments directly to you as defined by their product brochure.

- Each annuity product offers a basic death benefit. This means that if you die during the time the annuity is growing (the accumulation period), a deferred annuity will pay some or all of the annuity's value to your beneficiaries in one payment or in multiple payments over time. The amount paid to you will be the annuity account value, or if the account has not yet reached the end of the guaranteed surrender period, the guaranteed surrender value indicated for the year in which you die. You will receive whichever benefit is greater.

- If you die after you begin receiving annuity income payments, meaning you have annuitized your account, your

beneficiaries may not receive anything unless: 1) your annuity guarantees that the insurance company will pay out at
least as much as you put into the annuity, or 2) you choose
a payout option that continues to make payments to your
beneficiaries after you die. If you want this feature, ask for
the Enhanced Death Benefits Rider, which increases the
value of the basic death benefit.

- Insurance companies usually pay the annuity salesperson
  after the sale, but the payment doesn't reduce the amount
  you've paid into your annuity.

- The annuity strategy is a great way to create multiple sources of income and you can layer them so they become available at different times during your retirement.

- Many investors prefer the stability and relative safety of the
  guaranteed return provided by annuities. With annuities, you
  are not subject to volatile market swings like you are in stocks.

Annuity Terms

Here are four terms you'll hear frequently while discussing your
annuity with your salesperson:

- **Contract:** The legal document between you and the insurance company that binds both of you to the terms of the
  agreement.

- **Disclosure:** A document that describes the key features of
  your annuity, including what is guaranteed and what isn't,
  and your annuity's fees and charges. If you buy a variable
  annuity, you'll receive a prospectus that includes detailed
  information about investment objectives, risks, charges,
  and expenses.

- **Illustration:** A personalized document that shows how your annuity features might work. Be sure to ask what is guaranteed and what isn't and what assumptions were made when creating the illustration.

- **Annuitization:** When you annuitize, you tell the insurance company to start paying you by submitting a form. When providing these instructions, you'll need to decide exactly how the payments should be structured, and several different options may exist. You can find them in your contract or call the insurance company for assistance.

You may be thinking, *This sounds really good, but there has to be some disadvantage*, and you're right. There are disadvantages. Like everything, we need to figure out the advantages and disadvantages before making a decision.

Deferred Annuities and Their Disadvantages

- Annuity income will be taxed just like ordinary income, so there is a chance that your tax rate could go up between now and the time you want your annuity to start paying out.

- Annuities may restrict your flexibility since early withdrawal often means paying a penalty. Experts refer to this as illiquidity. Some annuities do allow penalty-free partial withdrawals or disability/hardship exceptions.

- Some annuity owners have pointed out that annuities may restrict the investment options available and saddle investors with limited choices in exchange for safety. This is because there are surrender charges. However, there are times when you'll sleep better knowing that you can't lose your money and that it's growing without concern.

- There are fees. There are no fees to roll your money over, but there are fees if you select a rider, giving you extra benefits protection or providing a lifetime income.

Differences in Deferred Annuities

There are two types of deferred annuities: fixed or variable. How the value of an annuity changes and grows is different depending on whether it is fixed or variable. The National Association of Insurance Commissioners describes these annuities as follows:

> *Fixed annuities* guarantee your money will earn at least a minimum interest rate. They may earn interest at a rate higher than the minimum but only the minimum rate is guaranteed unless you add the rider to the basic policy. [In this case, the rate is determined as noted in the policy rider brochure and the lifetime rider provides a lifetime payout. I always select this rider for my clients so that they'll receive a monthly income when they decide to stop working.]
>
> *Fixed Indexed annuities* earn interest based on changes in a market index, which measures how the market or a part of the market performs. The interest rate is guaranteed to never be less than zero, even if the market goes down.
>
> *Variable annuities* provide investment returns based on the performance of the investment portfolios, known as "subaccounts." When you invest your money in a Variable Annuity, it will be in a subaccount. The return earned in a variable annuity isn't guaranteed. The value of the subaccounts you choose could go up or down. If they go up, you could make money. But if the value of the subaccounts goes down, you could lose money. This strategy makes it difficult to plan for your future because the payments are subject to the market and you may receive less than you expected.

Some annuities give you a premium bonus, which is normally a lump sum amount from the insurance company. The bonus monies are added to you're annuity when you deposit your money into the account. It's usually a percentage of the amount you put into the annuity. Other annuities provide an interest bonus, which is an amount the insurance company adds to your annuity when interest is earned.

Rolling Qualified Funds into a Roth IRA Annuity

A Roth IRA is an individual retirement account that allows a person to set aside after-tax income up to a specified amount each year. Both earnings on the account and withdrawals after age 58½ are tax free because you've already paid the taxes on these funds.

In 1997, Delaware Senator William Victor Roth II proposed this type of investment account to Congress.

Some people ask me, "Why not take my money out of my 401k and put it in a Roth IRA? Then it will grow and I won't have to pay taxes on it." That's an interesting idea, but you may want to take into consideration these three consequences:

1. When you convert from a Traditional IRA to a Roth IRA, you pay income taxes on the contributions. The taxable amount that is converted is added to your income taxes and your regular income rate is applied to your total income.

2. Paying taxes on your entire account, all at one time, devalues your savings so you don't have the same value and growing power to invest your money in other strategies. Reinvesting in your qualified account and then taking smaller payments toward your monthly income can be considered one of your multiple streams of income and trigger smaller tax payments.

3. Taxable events can be an unnecessary surprise. Before moving forward with rolling your money out of a qualified funds account into a Roth IRA, check with your accountant. Doing so may cause you to step up into a higher tax bracket that will cost you thousands of dollars you wouldn't otherwise have been liable for.

If you anticipate your income dropping significantly in a certain year (and increasing in following years), you could plan a conversion for the low-income year. Since your income is lower, you may be in a lower tax bracket when you convert.

You must be separated from your employer to roll your 401k into a Roth IRA or any other account outside the company 401k perimeters. Most companies won't allow their company administrator to roll employees out of their 401k plan.

Whom do you know who would like to double his or her savings safely? I hope you have your hand up. There are products that will create much better earnings and a safer return with guarantees than a 401k. We don't plan to fail; we simply aren't always aware that there are products that provide safety and growth.

In this chapter, we've looked at some of the safest ways to invest. Of course, there are many more options and opportunities to research. In fact, there are so many that entire books have been written on this one topic. It might be considerably easier to discuss these ideas with your financial advisor, if you have one, and, of course, you can always contact me directly for more information. There are also account managers at the banks who can set you up with a CD or IRA rollover if that's an easier way for you to go.

One of the biggest challenges is that you might not be sure whether doing an IRA rollover is the right thing for you. Have you ever felt lost when it comes to your finances? Many of my clients tell me, "I've been working toward having security in my later years, but I'm not sure about where I am right now in the process and what might be missing. I wish I had a plan to follow." Others tell me they don't have enough money to plan right now so they'll worry about it later. That's a really bad plan. It's when you don't have the money that you need to plan your way into more money and a secure future.

If you'd like to discover where you stand on your financial path, I'm offering those who read my book the opportunity to take the Dreams Score™ Profile and get a FREE financial report. It is fully automated and does a great job of pointing out where you are in the process and what you need to do to get on track. It takes about ten minutes to complete and you'll get an instant report after you've finished answering the questions. You can start by going to my website at ShirleneReeves.com and clicking on the Financial Freedom button.

In the next chapter, I'll share with you my favorite strategy for financial security. It takes time to implement, but if you keep this strategy in the back of your mind, you'll find that you'll never again experience the feeling of lack because money will always show up from somewhere at any given time. Are you curious? Well then, read on.

"How many millionaires do you know who have become wealthy by investing in savings accounts? I rest my case."

— Robert G. Allen

♡

CHAPTER 24

Maximizing Wealth Formula

Twenty years ago, Robert Allen wrote the book *Multiple Steams of Income*, which went on to become a #1 *New York Times* bestseller. Recently, I interviewed Robert on my WMAX.TV show. During that interview, he said, "Some people read the book and do nothing and some put it into action. You are one of those who put it into action." I did put it into action and I believe that everyone should put this information into action. You can watch more of his interview on my website http://maximizeyourwealthnow.com/robertallen.

When I read Robert's book, it became clear that if multiple streams of income could be established within my business, I could teach other entrepreneurs how to create multiple streams of income for themselves. This one strategy keeps money flowing in from many different directions, creating security while you sleep.

Everybody needs multiple streams of income. If you only have one stream of income and you lose it, you'll end up broke or in the unemployment line. However, if you have a number of different avenues of income, you will always be safe and financially secure because the loss of one stream won't have much of an impact on your lifestyle.

The idea is to create streams of income that pay you while you sleep. Robert Allen says that we should keep this thought as a permanent part of our mindset, and that's what I chose to do at a very young age.

It's not always easy to create these streams of income, but anyone and everyone can do it if you simply keep it in mind and think about how to create them. If you have a job, start a business on the side. This gives you a tax advantage, and since we have no control or stability in holding a job, a business would be your fallback position.

When looking at the many ways of earning an income, ask yourself, "Will this other source of income I'm creating be a job that requires me to be there full-time? If you need to be there night and day, you've created another job for yourself. The idea is to create streams of income that will perpetuate without you being there every moment. Yes, you need to oversee the numbers and maintain them, but they are not just another job that takes up your time and energy.

There are many ways to make money while you sleep. Robert Allen names ten ideas in his book, such as real estate, network marketing, the stock market, licensing your own products, and a number of others. The idea is to figure out which streams resonate with you. I started by adding one, and once I got that one going, I added another and another. This way, if I lose one, I'll have four others that provide income.

As a business owner, with programs to sell, you can finance those programs for your clients and generate a monthly income that is consistent just like the companies I mentioned earlier in the exercise "uncovering unnecessary expenses." Those companies have it all figured out. If you elect to utilize their service, you are required to pay them every month, and that feeds a guaranteed income to support their business. Some call those streams of income bloodlines because they are the cash that keeps the company going.

Why not follow their lead and provide payment plans for your clients? When you finance a program for your clients, you can add an additional 15 percent for the finance and processing costs and then break the payments out for six months, providing a stream of income that is paid automatically every month for six months. If you have a lot of students, you'll have a lot of monthly income even if you didn't make a sale that month.

I also discuss this theory with my financial clients who want to receive streams of income at a time when they no longer want to work so hard. It's just about impossible to amass millions in the bank to live off of in our later years and so much easier to develop multiple streams of income that come in automatically every month. This can be set up through annuities, life insurance policies, Social Security (as long as it lasts), real estate investments, and residuals. If you've created licensing certifications in your business or are receiving royalties, those will also provide a substantial income for you.

I enjoy looking at the lifestyles of my clients, formulating a plan for multiple streams of income, and then watching them make money while they sleep, travel, and enjoy their lives. We can talk about creating multiple streams of income for you during your free forty-minute financial consultation. Wouldn't you love to make money while you sleep? I sure do.

List five possible streams of income that you can work toward developing. Remember the rules:

1. Get one stream of income up and running at a time before moving onto the next.

2. Don't create a stream of income that requires you to work full-time. (You don't want another job.)

3. Watch over the numbers for each stream carefully.

4. Look for possible licensing and residual income based on products and services you already provide.

5. Make sure you have a minimum of four streams when you decide to do nothing but travel and play.

1. _____

   _____

2. _____

   _____

3. _____

   _____

4. _____

   _____

5. _____

   _____

When I sit down with seniors, or people in their mid-fifties, they are devastated at the amount of money they "should" have in the bank to retire. They often say that it's so costly to live their lives on a monthly basis that there's been no additional income to add to savings. Aside from that, there is no substantial amount of interest offered at the banks to make a savings account worthwhile other than providing for an emergency fund. "So what can I do?" they ask. "I always said I'd never retire, but I was lying to myself. I'm done." This is when we look seriously at how they can live comfortably on multiple streams of income.

There was a day when the interest at the banks was so high that people could live on the interest without touching the principal savings amount, but those days are gone. *So, what do we do now?* you might be wondering. You develop multiple streams of income.

1. If you are 59½, you can start to draw off of your 401k and IRA monies.

2. When you are 67, you will begin receiving Social Security if you live in the United States and have been paying into your Social Security account.

3. Hopefully, you've acquired an annuity that provides a rider with lifetime income.

4. You'll receive tax-free income from your life insurance if you choose a policy with those provisions.

5. If you own a house, you can apply for a reverse mortgage for up to 60 percent of the value of your house, less the mortgage and any necessary repairs. A reverse mortgage allows you to continue ownership of your home to continue living in it, and you may elect to receive monthly, annual, or lump sum payments, which you can use for anything you wish. After you die or if you live away from your home for a year or more, you'll be required either to sell or offer it to your children for purchase to payback the reverse mortgage. You or your heirs will also receive the 40 percent in equity plus any increases in value.

6. If you've acquired a vacation rental or second home, it can be rented out for additional income.

Bonus Thought: Rent one of your rooms out on Airbnb. I did it for two years, made approximately $1,000 a month or more, and it lowered the amount I paid for my apartment. These are just a few ideas and there are so many more. The myriad of investment opportunities and ideas for added income are limitless. I've even invested in property that includes a Deed of Trust in Mexico. It's called a speculation land buy. As I write these words, the land is still ridiculously inexpensive. A quarter acre developed lot for $7,000, with an ocean view, is an amazing buy, and it won't last. The city of San Felipe is already making improvements, and like the increases in Cabo land, we're speculating that each lot will go up to $100,000, adding a nice little pot of income to my multiple steams of income.

What are your thoughts about living the lifestyle you want to live later in life? Opportunities shift and change consistently, so keep your eyes open, investigate thoroughly, and know that the old adage, "If it sounds too good to be true it probably is" may not be the best policy to live by. Sometimes we need to jump in and take the risk. Those who do are the ones who live comfortably later in life, and you can be one of them. Check it out for yourself and then decide.

I've given you a lot to think about in this chapter. But I'd suggest that you consider what it means for you to live comfortably. Many people say they want to live a great lifestyle, but they make no effort to get there and, in fact, they haven't even considered what their comfort level is. Start by defining specifically and realistically what you envision your life to look like, and then begin thinking about the cost of that lifestyle. Are you willing to be a minimalist, or is travel in your future? Remember when I said, "We don't plan to fail. We just fail to plan." This is your opportunity to plan your future and how you intend to reach your desired goals.

♡

FINAL NOTE

Winning the Entrepreneurial Game

In your hands, you have the benefit of my twenty-eight years of knowledge tacking back and forth to reach new heights in business. Now it's your turn to make the same decision I did twenty-nine years ago. Are you going to end up under a bridge and take the *dive*, or *ditch* the feeling of confusion and accept the clarity provided be-tween the covers of this book? Only you can change the way you look at things and take the steps necessary to become one of the 20 percent of entrepreneurs who excel in business. See you at the top!

> *"Some people read a book and do nothing*
> *and some put it into action."*
>
> — Robert G. Allen

Which one are you?

Now is the time to take the steps necessary to prosper and build sales revenue. What goals have you set up for yourself? Which steps have you overlooked? What is your intention, and by when will you achieve it?

If you haven't completed the list below, take the time now to review the chapters again. Check each box as you complete the items on the path of your business blueprint. For those you haven't finished yet, write down next to it the date by which you will commit to finishing it.

- ☐ Identify your target market.
- ☐ Use the words and phrases your clients are waiting to hear.
- ☐ Practice by opening authentic sales conversations.
- ☐ Build confidence in front of the camera.
- ☐ Develop your massive visibility media message.
- ☐ Create your 5-7 word tagline.
- ☐ Design and memorize your thirty-second networking pitch.
- ☐ Close sales and give referrals to community members.
- ☐ Understand who you are as a salesperson and how to relate to other personality types.
- ☐ Paint client dreams with benefits for better sales results.
- ☐ Define authentic words and phrases that speak to your perfect clients.
- ☐ Act on the secrets to successful networking.
- ☐ Practice the easy sales close.
- ☐ Understand the purpose of media visibility for sales success.
- ☐ Put safe and successful financial strategies into practice.
- ☐ Capture the lifestyle you deserve by making money while you sleep.

Knowledge is not power. Only applied knowledge is power. You can read this book from cover to cover, but if you don't apply the step-by-step process, you'll be in the exact same place as you were when you read the introduction.

Clarity, confidence, visibility, and income are the four pillars of understanding and accomplishment we work toward together in Compel Don't Sell™: The Art of Selling With Heart, Business Mastery Platinum and Massive Visibility Media™ courses. Each class stands on its own, and there is an in-depth description of each on the pages that follow.

This is your book. It complements the courses perfectly, and it's designed to be a reference guide to keep you on track while walking the path of your newly developed business blueprint. Write your Big Business Vision below, remembering that now is the time to dream big and let the universe know what you desire.

When you enter your vision below, you are sending a personal message of agreement to the universe that you are dedicated to empowering yourself, building the business of your dreams and living the lifestyle you deserve.

_____

_____

_____

_____

_____

Date: _____   Signature: _____

Remember when I asked what you'd do if you knew exactly how to win? Well, now you know how to win, so what will you do? You've learned the answers for determining who your target market is, where to find your clients, how to open a sales conversation authentically, how to make a sale without feeling pushy or getting rejected, and greatest of all, you've received a business blueprint and the secrets for building a profitable income-generating business.

WINNING THE ENTREPRENEURIAL GAME

You have in your hands the secrets for exactly how to win the entrepreneurial game. If you apply the wisdom, knowledge, skills, techniques, and strategies offered in this book toward your business, you most assuredly will achieve what *Selling Through Your Heart* promises: achieving a wonderful rich life with lots of heartfelt relationships wrapping you in financial freedom.

I encourage you to contact me and tell me what you liked or disliked about my book so I can improve it for the next printing. Your feedback is vitally important to me.

More importantly, tell me about you and your challenges so I can support you. In fact, I would like to offer you a complimentary, no obligation forty-minute consultation by phone, Skype, or in person (if geography allows) so I can learn how I can support you and determine whether you are ready to become a "go-to" celebrity guest expert in your specialized area of expertise.

I'm hoping this book will be a new beginning for us. Now that you have this book in your hands, I hope it will become a resource that you review frequently so you can succeed as a massively visible entrepreneur on your way to achieving financial freedom.

My email address is sreeves@maximizeyourwealthnow.com and

my cell phone is 925-335-6077 so please email me, or better yet text me with your name and time zone, and we will schedule your complimentary consultation.

I wish you good luck! I wish you great success and a prosperous lifestyle! I wish you all the financial blessings and abundance in the world.

Warmly,

ABOUT THE AUTHOR

Shirlene Reeves is a Distinguished Toastmaster and international keynote speaker. She publishes *Wealthy Woman Magazine* and is a TV and syndicated radio show host.

As a massive visibility media™ educator, Shirlene blends business and financial strategies with universal principles. She strengthens your business and expands your vision through massive visibility.

Shirlene has a varied and balanced background, with education and experience in both financial and spiritual principles. On the financial side, she is one of only 253 CFE Certified Financial Educators® in the nation, and she has more than twenty-eight years of experience. She was the CEO of her own nationwide California C corporation for over seventeen years, which she bootstrapped from zero to millions with over 23,000 working under her.

Originally from San Jose, California, Shirlene has a Bachelor of Arts degree in sociology with a minor in psychology from California State University, San Jose (SJSU). While on Maui, she earned her Bachelor of Arts and master's degrees from the University of Metaphysics and trained with best-selling author and speaker Dr. Wayne Dyer and American spiritual teacher and former Harvard professor Ram Das.

Shirlene focuses on teaching CEOs and business owners how to shine on stage or in front of the camera to make a massive impact on their perfect demographic through her specialized classes.

Shirlene lives in San Diego, California with her little dog Deani, and she loves playing with her two young grandsons, Blake and Gavin. She travels all over the world, takes long walks on the beach, and makes frequent trips to her home on the beach in San Felipe, Baja California, Mexico.

MAXIMIZE YOUR WEALTH NOW BUSINESS COURSES

Clarity • **Confidence** • **Visibility** • **Income**

Why do some people succeed at levels beyond their imagination, while others struggle? It all comes down to how they develop and manage their business productivity and relationship skills. Think about it: If you haven't mastered the necessary sales skills that will prepare you for generating an income, building relationship referrals, and confidently influencing others to purchase your programs, products, or services, then you're stuck forever in mediocrity. But if you can master those skills, then your life changes forever and your business soars.

Shirlene believes that the Goal of a Great Teacher is to Awaken the Awareness of the Greatness in Others.

To awaken that awareness in you, Shirlene offers three courses:

Compel Don't Sell™: The Art of Selling with Heart

Business Mastery Platinum

Massive Visibility Media™ Gold

Find out more on the following pages.

COMPEL DON'T SELL: THE ART OF SELLING WITH HEART FOUR-MONTH COURSE

Eight students of the Compel Don't Sell course made sales totaling:

- $108,444 in only 8 weeks
- $274,343 in only 9 weeks
- $301,180 in only 10 weeks

Compel Don't Sell is one of the most incredible personal development sales seminars in the world. It's entirely different from anything you've ever experienced before because it includes new, modern sales techniques perfected by Shirlene Reeves over twenty-eight years. In this course, you will learn first about your own personality in the sales process, and then you will focus on how best to work with converting prospects into long-term clients. It's perfect for small business owners, coaches, and speakers just starting their new careers or for advanced business owners who have been struggling with the inefficiency and inauthenticity of the old way of doing sales.

Here's a glimpse at what you'll get when you say "Yes" to Compel Don't Sell:

- Learn the 3 Step Sales Waltz™ to Sales Success.
- Zero in on Your Perfect Clients.
- Easily Overcome Objections, Rejection, and Feeling Pushy.
- Speak the Words Your Clients Are Waiting to Hear.
- Discover How to Open a Sales Conversation Easily.
- Learn the Secret to Caring Client Retention.
- Discover Where to Find Your Clients.
- Profile Yourself as a Salesperson and Acquire the Art of Engaging With Heart.

- Engage Confidently and Authentically in the Sales Process Without Scripts.
- Attend the Ninety-Day Weekly Group Coaching Sales Boot Camp.

Compel Don't Sell is one of the most life-changing and unique courses, incorporating the latest and most effective strategies and tools in personal growth, positive psychology, relationship growth, and high performance.

To watch student testimonials, visit:
http://maximizeyourwealthnow.com/compel-dont-sell/

BUSINESS MASTERY PLATINUM
BUILD AN EMPIRE AND CAREER BY MONETIZING WHAT YOU KNOW

SIX-MONTH COURSE. INCLUDES STUDENT MASTERMIND AND ONE-ON-ONE COACHING

Have you ever felt like you're running from one networking group to another, working hard to make an income, and still you aren't seeing the results you'd hoped for? Have you ever stumbled through explanations when clients ask, "What do you do?" Are you trying to figure out what to do with your lifetime of skills and how to integrate them into your business programs?

If these challenges sound familiar, you may be on the verge of burnout and frustration. A setback is a great time for a comeback, and the Business Mastery Platinum course is a great place to stop the spinning and focus on what it takes to up-level your business and start generating an income. This course is the perfect complement to the highly acclaimed Compel Don't Sell: The Art of Selling With Heart course where eight students made $301,000 in only ten weeks.

- Pinpoint your target market to save time, stop spinning, and overcome frustration and burnout.

- Define the benefits of the product or service you provide for client clarity.

- Determine networking groups that generate great sales leads for practicing the 3 Step Sales Waltz™.

- Discover "Hey, she gets me" words and phrases your clients are waiting to hear.

- Design three integrated, well-developed programs for easier client sales.

- Create sensational seminar content that your clients will love.

- Learn how to maintain client retention and referrals to generate more income.

- Create a 5-7 word tagline that defines your business succinctly and elicits client lean-in.
- Dive deeper into the DISC sales process for better client communication.
- Develop your thirty-second networking promo.
- Attend our massive visibility online zoom weekly mastermind group with community support while developing programs and defining proper pricing.

To watch student testimonials, visit:
http://maximizeyourwealthnow.com/business-mastery

MASSIVE VISIBILITY MEDIA™ GOLD

ADVANCED PERFORMANCE AND PROMOTIONS TRAINING FOR TOMORROW'S GREAT SPEAKERS

A FOUR-MONTH MEDIA GROWTH EXPERIENCE.
INCLUDES STUDENT MASTERMIND

Shirlene Reeves is one of the most highly visible business leaders and media trainers in the world. She has interviewed greats such as Robert Allen, Dr. John Demartini, and D. C. Cordova on her *WMAX.TV* show and her *Ascended Masters at Work* syndicated radio show. Shirlene teaches you how to become more confident on camera, build your own home studio, create your own videos, and start your own talk show. Shirlene will show you how to master today's necessary skills so you can become tomorrow's expert media speaker.

If you already have a solid business foundation, integrated programming, and little if any challenge selling and generating an income, you are ready for the Massive Visibility Media™ Course.

Have you ever felt like you're playing in a pool of people that is way too small? Shirlene felt that way once. She spent all of her time networking with people in her local area, and she soon found that her little pool needed to become an ocean of sales possibilities. That's why she became massively visible and can now teach you to do the same.

Once you've taken this course, you'll leap out of your own backyard and make a massive difference in the world and in your income. This course is designed for entrepreneurs and coaches with a solid business foundation, integrative programming, and little if any challenge selling and generating an income. If you haven't yet reached this goal, you may find the world-renowned Compel Don't Sell course and the Business Mastery Platinum course perfect prerequisites to prepare you for this intensive four-month media growth experience.

Here's how you'll learn to double your income through this course:

- Become a sought-after celebrity guest expert.
- Professionally represent your industry on web TV, podcasts, and syndicated radio shows.
- Present yourself professionally with style.
- Practice building confidence in front of the camera.
- Learn to speak in three-minute sound bites.
- Create your own professional videos.
- Learn techniques for working with Zoom, YouTube, and Facebook.
- Create two-minute videos that provide weekly database awareness.
- Get a free list of promoters looking for speakers.
- Learn skills for on-the-spot interviews.
- Create your own home studio for a professional appearance.
- Get an equipment list and step-by-step set up instructions with lighting and camera tips.
- Join the massive visibility elite community, working together to increase business sales.

To watch student testimonials, visit:

http://maximizeyourwealthnow.com/massive-visibility

DISC SALES ONLINE REPORT
FIND OUT WHY YOUR CLIENTS BUY

Discover the secrets to selling more effectively and efficiently by determining your own behavior patterns and how they relate to others. Easily identify personalities and how to communicate effectively with them to create more and better sales conversations. Open sales conversations with confidence and clarity. Download your report today and start selling like a pro tomorrow.

DISC Sales Report: Generate More Income for You and Your Business

This thirty-page report not only reveals your personal strengths and how to identify and adapt your own style when approaching your client, but it outlines a step-by-step strategy that allows you to customize your approach throughout the selling process. This report is the perfect companion for the Compel Don't Sell course. It is provided free when you take the course, but if you wish to take this profile on your own, you can buy it at ShirleneReeves.com.

DISC for Coaching: 20% OFF (use Coupon Code: Shirlene for limited time only offer)

If you are a coach, psychologist, therapist, or someone working on overcoming client challenges and their effects on your clients' lifestyles, this is a perfect certification for you. With this certification, you can provide better, quicker, and more effective solutions for your clients. They can pay for their profiles individually, or you can wrap the cost into your coaching fee like I do in my Compel Don't Sell course. When you are DISC Certified, you can ask your clients to take the DISC profile, receive an instant report, and provide spot-on coaching that gets to the root of your clients' challenges.

DISC for Leaders: DISCovering My Leadership Style

This forty-seven-page report not only reveals your personal strengths, but it provides ways to identify and adapt your own leadership style to provide what is needed to motivate, manage, acknowledge, and align others. This valuable report is ideal for all regional managers, directors, and corporate team members.

DISC For Self: DISCovering Me

This twenty-three-page report introduces you to your personal qualities, motivators, needs, and character virtue strengths. You will also learn about your communication preferences for interacting most effectively with others. If you are having challenges with family and friends, then taking this profile will provide you with the answers that will bring peace and better relationships into your life.

All DISC Reports can be purchased at ShirleneReeves.com

Join Our Elite International Community of Entrepreneurs Working Together to Lift Their Businesses Toward Making A Heartfelt Global Difference

BOOK SHIRLENE REEVES
TO SPEAK AT YOUR NEXT EVENT

When looking for a professional keynote speaker for your next event, you'll be hard-pressed to find anyone more highly respected and successful as a business, sales, and financial educator than Shirlene Reeves. She will leave your audience or colleagues with a renewed zest for business and financial success.

As a Distinguished Toastmaster, Shirlene is considered one of the most gifted speakers in the United States. Since 2005, she has produced more than 440 YouTube videos. She is the host of WMAX. TV on Voice America TV with over 4.3 million viewers, and she currently hosts a syndicated radio show on BBS radio.

Shirlene Reeves will deliver a relaxed, enjoyable educational message of inspiration and success. Whether your audience is 12 or 12,000, in North America or abroad, Shirlene understands the importance of relating a message to your audience that includes enlightening, real-life stories wrapped in teachable moments that include audience participation, humor, and entertainment. She is known for her passion, inspiration, and an uplifting educational style that achieves extraordinary results.

If you are looking for an enlightening speaker who will leave your audience desiring more, book Shirlene Reeves today!

To see highlight videos of Shirlene Reeves and find out whether she is available for your next meeting, visit her site at the address below. Then contact her by phone or email to schedule a complimentary pre-speech phone interview:

ShirleneReeves.com
SReeves@MaximizeYourWealthNow.com
Mobile: 925-335-6077